D0922548

WILLIAM BLAKE'S POETRY

CONTINUUM READER'S GUIDES

WILLIAM BLAKE'S POETRY

A Reader's Guide

JONATHAN ROBERTS

continuum

Continuum International Publishing Group
The Tower Building   80 Maiden Lane
11 York Road   Suite 704
London   New York
SE1 7NX   NY 10038

© Jonathan Roberts 2007

All rights reserved. No part of this publication may be reproduced or
transmitted in any form or by any means, electronic or mechanical,
including photocopying, recording, or any information storage or retrieval
system, without prior permission in writing from the publishers.

Jonathan Roberts has asserted his right under the Copyright, Designs and
Patents Act, 1988, to be identified as Author of this work.

British Library Cataloguing-in-Publication Data
A catalogue record for this book is available from the British Library.

ISBN – 10: 0 8264 8859 5 (hardback)
           0 8264 8860 9 (paperback)
ISBN – 13: 978 08264 8859 6 (hardback)
           978 08264 8860 2 (paperback)

Library of Congress Cataloging-in-Publication Data
A catalog record for this book is available from the Library of Congress.

Typeset by Servis Filmsetting Ltd, Manchester
Printed and bound in Great Britain by
MPG Books Ltd, Bodmin, Cornwall

In memory of Tim Cross (1970–97) – always delighted
with the enjoyments of genius

CONTENTS

ACKNOWLEDGEMENTS

Thanks to Colin Thorpe for introducing me to (among other things) Blake, Emma Mason for helpful scepticism over my image of Blake, and Chris Rowland for ongoing insight into my instrumental use of Blake. For helpful feedback on the manuscript, thanks to Jon Thorpe and Sue Wollen. For all the other support that let this book happen, to Keith and Carol Roberts, and to Ying Roberts, thanks.

NOTES ON SOURCES

This book relies on five reference works for the facts about Blake's life, work, book-making methods, and reception. These are:

Bentley, G. E. Jr, *The Stranger from Paradise* (New Haven: Yale University Press, 2001)

Bentley, G. E. Jr, *Blake Records*, second edition (New Haven: Yale University Press, 2004)

Dorfman, Deborah, *Blake in the Nineteenth Century* (New Haven: Yale University Press, 1969)

Erdman, David, *The Complete Poetry and Prose of William Blake*, newly revised edition (Anchor Books, 1988)

Viscomi, Joseph, *Blake and the Idea of the Book* (Princeton: Princeton University Press, 1993)

I have drawn extensively on Bentley's *The Stranger from Paradise* for biography; Bentley's *Blake Records* for other material pertaining to Blake's life; Dorfman's *Blake in the Nineteenth Century* for the reception of Blake in the Victorian period; Erdman's *Complete Poetry and Prose* as the standard edition of the writings; and Viscomi's *Blake and the Idea of the Book* for Blake's production methods. All references to *Bentley* are to *The Stranger from Paradise*, unless stated as *Blake Records*.

References to Blake works follow page numbers in Erdman, as, for example, *E*49. Where available, I have also included page or plate numbers (corresponding to the format in which Blake printed his works) in case the reader is using a different edition. The Erdman references have the advantage that they can be followed up online, as both the text itself, and an electronic concordance of the edition are available at http://www.english.uga.edu/wblake. In addition, Blake's illuminated books along with a host of other materials can be viewed online at www.blakearchive.org.

Blake uses idiosyncratic punctuation and spelling which can sometimes make his meaning difficult to grasp. For the sake of clarity in this introductory work, I have occasionally amended Blake's punctuation and spelling in order to make the quotations more immediately accessible. Although these are minor changes, they constitute an act of interpretation, and all quotations therefore need to be read against the original texts.

References to websites are contained in endnotes. All references to other printed works are in the form of (author, page number) after the relevant quotation; further details can then be found in Works Cited. All biblical quotations are from the NIV (New International Version). Parts of Chapter 3 appeared previously in an article entitled 'St Paul's Gift to Blake's Aesthetic', published in *The Glass*, 15 (2003).

This book is in six parts. Chapter 1 gives an account of Blake's life along with basic introductions to the political, social, intellectual and religious movements that influenced his works. Chapter 2 gives a similar introductory account to the aesthetic, poetic and artistic movements that shaped the form of his art. The third chapter gives an account of the major themes and philosophical ideas of Blake's work in conjunction with reference to a wide range of his poems. The fourth chapter describes critical responses to Blake from the nineteenth to the twenty-first century, and this account is broadened in the fifth chapter into a description of Blake's impact on later artists and his cultural adoption by, for example, proponents of psychoactive drugs. Chapter 6, the final chapter, offers a thematically organized guide to further reading.

The first two chapters present a large amount of information pertaining to Blake's life and contexts with limited discussion of his actual ideas and work. It is Chapter 3, 'Reading Blake', that offers close and sustained engagement with these matters. Each chapter is followed by a few study questions which are designed to connect the discussion back to Blake's most commonly read works, *The Songs of Innocence and of Experience* and *The Marriage of Heaven and Hell*.

CHAPTER 1

CONTEXTS

BLAKE AS A ROMANTIC

Blake was considerably older than the other traditional 'Romantics':
13 years older than Wordsworth, 15 years than Coleridge, 31 years
than Byron, and 38 years than Keats. Compared to the lives of these
contemporaries – Byron, Shelley, or even the young Wordsworth –
Blake's life was mundane. He was born in London on 28 November
1757, and, with the exception of three years living on the south coast
of England (1800–3), stayed there until his death in 1827. He
suffered no early bereavements, never joined the army, never left
England, never went to university, never went on the Grand Tour,
did not have a string of failed relationships or lovers, didn't take
opium, wasn't in France during the Revolution, fathered no children, never became famous during his own lifetime, worked steadily
at his profession to support himself and his wife, and died peacefully
in (what at the time was considered) old age. His art is made from
whatever came to hand, not only contemporary social and political
events, but domestic matters including his acquaintances, his home
life, his own engraving procedures, and so on. From the dark fusion
of his mind, these phenomena re-emerge as terrible gods, visions of
the dead, spirits of joy, the suffering and dispossessed calling forth
judgement on the powers that be. His art cannot be explained by
these contexts, but knowledge of them can make his work more
accessible. It is these contexts that the first two chapters describe
before looking at the operation of his art more closely in Chapter 3.

EARLY LIFE: EDUCATION AND 'VISIONS'

Blake's father ran a hosiery and haberdashery shop in Westminster, London. His parents appear to have been gentle people, interested in their children (and willing to support, for example, Blake's wish to attend drawing school), and both survived well into Blake's adulthood. Blake had an elder brother, two younger brothers, and a younger sister. He was not sent to school (free public education for all children was still over a century away), but in his earlier childhood was educated at home by his mother. His life at this time was undramatic, and without obvious trauma. The only marked peculiarity was that from an early age Blake 'saw visions'. G. E. Bentley Jr, pre-eminent collector and disseminator of information on Blake's life and contexts, writes:

> From his earliest childhood Blake saw visions. When he was four years old, God put his head to the window and set the child screaming, and once "his mother beat him for running in & saying that he saw the Prophet Ezekiel under a Tree in the Fields." Later, when he was eight or ten, one day as he was walking on Peckham Rye [. . .] he saw "a tree filled with angels, bright angelic wings bespangling every bough like stars." When he told this story at home, it was "only through his mother's intercession . . . [*that he escaped*] a thrashing from his honest father for telling a lie." Another time, on a summer morning he saw "the hay-makers at work, and amid them angelic figures walking".
>
> (*Bentley*, 19–20)

Most biographers have accepted these stories, and – as Bentley does here – reported them in a matter-of-fact way, describing Blake as a 'visionary' rather than, say, suffering from psychosis. It's difficult to know what to make of such narratives, but it is important to note that they invariably come from other, later sources, and not directly from Blake himself. Any judgement on these matters should also take into account the following three things. First, Blake deploys such 'visions' in a self-consciously literary way in his writing, as, for example, when he reports in *The Marriage of Heaven and Hell* that 'The Prophets Isaiah and Ezekiel dined with me' (pl. 12, *E*37): here Blake is giving a tongue-in-cheek account of the two untameable

EARLY ENCOUNTERS WITH STATE VIOLENCE

By the time Blake was beginning to write, well over two centuries had passed since the establishment of the Church of England, and more than a century since the English Civil War (1642–51). Nevertheless, tensions between religious denominations in England and their connection to politics and social unrest were still strongly evident, not least because dissent was legislated against through the Test and Corporation Acts which were not repealed until after Blake's death. Blake's first personal encounter with just how strong these tensions could be – in the form of mob violence and subsequent state intervention – is likely to have been the Gordon Riots of 1780. The riots took place in response to new legislation (the Roman Catholic Relief Act of 1778) that gave Catholics fuller social rights. Lord George Gordon (President of the Protestant Association) organized a petition against the Act which led in turn to a huge demonstration at the Houses of Parliament. The situation became violent and, over the following days, there was extensive rioting and Catholic properties were attacked. The army was subsequently brought in and about 300 rioters were killed, with a further 30 or so executed thereafter. Blake was close to the centre of events (*Bentley*, 56), and saw first-hand both the power of mobs to destroy, and the power of the government to subsequently crush and punish those involved in mob action. The Gordon Riots did not, however, present an isolated incident of government oppression. They took place against a scene of international violence that had been underway for several years by this time: the American Revolution.

The American Revolution (1775–83) had been instigated by American colonists who wanted to gain independence from British rule, principally in response to high levels of taxation and lack of political representation. Moreover, some of these colonists came from families who had left Europe in the first place in order to escape its intolerance of their religious practices. The Revolution instigated the War of American Independence, and Blake – who was in his early twenties at the time – was very conscious of these events: the conscripts and discharged soldiers in London provided images that would subsequently inform poems such as 'London' (*E*25) where 'the hapless Soldier's sigh | Runs in blood down Palace walls': a poetic moment in which Blake pours the blood of English soldiers

Hebrew prophets sitting down to an eighteenth-century dinner party. Second, Blake often states that the act of perception involves an act of interpretation (see the end of *A Vision of The Last Judgment*, *E*564–5): what we see is influenced by who we are or, as Blake puts it, 'as a man is, So he sees' (*E*701). Third, he may have used his 'visions' playfully in the company of gullible friends such as John Varley (*Bentley*, 368ff), the astrologer for whom Blake drew 'visionary' portraits such as 'The Ghost of a Flea'. It is possible that Blake believed he had seen such things, but they may equally express a wicked sense of delight in pandering to the gullible.

The response of Blake's parents was also important to his development. In the case of the particular accounts described above, Blake's parents are shown to oppose the boy's visions, and he is depicted as a sort of junior prophet who is rejected in his own home. Generally speaking, however, Blake's parents were remarkably encouraging towards him, and when he showed an early interest in drawing, he was sent, aged ten, to Henry Pars' drawing school, which he attended until he was 14, during which time he also began writing poetry. At that point Blake's father made the significant investment in apprenticing Blake to a professional engraver, James Basire. It might have been anticipated that Blake would go into his father's business, but the apprenticeship again shows the willingness of Blake's parents to support him in following his talents. Blake's apprenticeship to Basire lasted seven years, during which time he learned the many technical skills necessary to engraving and etching, as well as making studies (as he had with Henry Pars) of prints and sculptures – including those at Westminster Abbey – that would substantially influence his later work. The apprenticeship was a full-time occupation and Blake lived with Basire, working six days a week. At the end of the training, he returned home to live with his family once more.

This account of Blake's formal education gives some indication of how he developed his artistic skills, but little explanation of the mix of radical politics and religion that suffuses his work. That requires short explanations of a different aspect of his education: his parents' religious position, and the political and social contexts within which he encountered these beliefs.

CONTEMPORARY RELIGION AND STATE POWER

Blake was a non-conformist. 'Non-conformism' refers historically to religious groups that had separated from the Church of England during the seventeenth and eighteenth centuries. The Church of England had its origins in the English Reformation, which was England's peculiar official conversion to Protestantism following Henry VIII's decision to separate his nation's church from that of Rome. These events foregrounded the principle of self-determination in religious worship and belief, and this characteristic would remain central to religious debate in England even after the Church of England was established in 1559 under Elizabeth I. One of the characteristics of the Reformation was that many groups and individuals, especially on the left-wing of the reformation, the so-called 'radical reformation' considered that the 'magesterial reformation' had not gone far enough. They wanted self-determination disagreeing with the theology and practices of the new state church. Such groups were called 'dissenters' or 'non-conformists', and in the years to come many of them would form religious communities of their own, including Puritans, Quakers, Baptists, Methodists and Unitarians. Because of the alliance of state power and state religion (the reigning English monarch was, and continues to be, the Supreme Governor of the Church of England), there was often a close correlation between religious dissent and political dissent: these non-conformists were people who didn't want the government telling them how to worship or what to believe or, by extension, how to live or what to think. There was, of course, a great range here: some of these groups, such as the Methodists, did not at first seek official separation from the Church of England, whereas other groups found the situation in Europe so intolerable that they emigrated to America in order to be able to practise their religious beliefs in the way that they felt necessary. The inseparability of politics and religion in Blake's England makes the seemingly forthright attacks on 'the Church' in his work more complex than they first seem, and means that they should not necessarily be identified as attacks on the Bible, Christianity, Jesus or religion, all of which signify quite different things.

There is an ongoing debate about the religious position of Blake's parents and their status as non-conformists, but it now seems very likely that his mother came from Nottinghamshire and was a

member (before marrying Blake's father) of the Moravian Ch a protestant denomination with its origins in (what is nov Czech Republic. Blake's parents' beliefs meant that he didn't church as a child. Moreover, he may have inherited a symbolic ious language which fused sexual and religious imagery. This can give a first taste of the radical nature of Blake's imaginatio is evident in the shocking notebook poem 'I saw a chapel all of in which a transgressive scene of penetrative sex is figured in of a phallic serpent bursting open the doors of a chapel, slidi the aisle, and vomiting onto the altar. In the first stanza, 'wi means 'outside', and in the final stanza, 'I turned into a sty' 'I went into a pig sty':

> I saw a chapel all of gold
> That none did dare to enter in
> And many weeping stood without
> Weeping mourning worshipping
>
> I saw a serpent rise between
> The white pillars of the door
> And he forced & forced & forced
> Down the golden hinges tore
>
> And along the pavement sweet
> Set with pearls & rubies bright
> All his slimy length he drew
> Till upon the altar white
>
> Vomiting his poison out
> On the bread & on the wine
> So I turned into a sty
> And laid me down among the swine (E466–7)

Why would Blake write such a poem? It puts its finger on th institutional powers (religion and state) attempt to control se through moral codes, and thereby inadvertently make it source of violence and degradation. We shall look at institu powers further in Chapter 3.

over the walls of the head of state, graphically reconnecting ideological responsibility and consequent human suffering. Likewise, the actions of George III and Washington (the leaders, respectively, of the English and American forces) would eventually be given mythical form by Blake in his work *America: A Prophecy*. Here, in the opening lines of the prophecy, Blake depicts the stand-off between the English and American leaders:

> The Guardian Prince of Albion burns in his nightly tent,
> Sullen fires across the Atlantic glow to America's shore:
> Piercing the souls of warlike men, who rise in silent night,
> Washington, Franklin, Paine & Warren, Gates, Hancock & Green;
> Meet on the coast glowing with blood from Albion's fiery Prince.
> (Pl. 3, *E*51)

The political leaders have here become mythological figures in a literary epic. In the early 1780s, however, these works were still a decade away, and this was a period during which Blake was beginning to establish his independence both domestically and as an artist. After serving his apprenticeship he became a student engraver at the Royal Academy, where he embarked on a programme which included lectures, drawing from sculptures, and life drawing (*Bentley*, 49). Alongside this study he was also doing professional work, engraving plates for commercial publishers.

MARRIAGE, SOCIAL CONNECTIONS, BUSINESS

In 1782 Blake married Catherine Boucher, whom he would subsequently teach to read and write, and to help in the production of his illuminated books. The couple had no children, but remained together until Blake's death, and biographies of Blake have often been enlivened by stories of the couple sitting naked in their garden reading *Paradise Lost*. Sadly, there is no evidence to bear this out, but it is true that Blake wrote some surprising things about marriage, such as:

> In a wife I would desire
> What in whores is always found
> The lineaments of Gratified desire (*E*473)

Here Blake again touches on the psychological impact of society's codification of sex. Attempting to legislate human love and sexuality leads, in Blake's view, to secret, shameful and illicit forms of sexuality. As he writes in one of the 'Proverbs of Hell', 'Prisons are built with stones of Law, Brothels with bricks of Religion' (*E*35). For this reason, and because Blake's work is sometimes interpreted as antinomian (that is, rejecting moral law), there has been much speculation over Blake's ideas about 'free love'. Whatever their concept of marriage was, however, contemporaries saw Blake and Catherine as a happy couple, and after 20 years of marriage a contemporary wrote, 'They . . . are as fond of each other, as if their Honey Moon were still shining . . . they seem animated by one Soul, & that a soul of indefatigable Industry & Benevolence' (quoted in *Bentley*, 69–70).

Blake's social circle was expanding at this time too, and he developed an important friendship with Reverend Anthony Mathew and his wife Harriet. The Mathews had money and education, and Harriet Mathew held parties to encourage artistic and intellectual discussion, as was common at the time. She welcomed Blake to her conversation groups, in which he sang his poems to an appreciative audience (*Bentley*, 74). Yet despite the encouragement that Blake received here, he was not quite on an equal footing with his hosts. There was a fad at this time for discovering 'untutored genius' – that is, artists who were not schooled but were 'natural': there was great interest, for example, in working-class writers such as Ann Yearsley, otherwise known as 'Lactilla, Milkwoman of Clifton'. Blake wasn't working-class (as an artisan he was somewhere between working- and middle-class), and he certainly wasn't untutored, but for his patrons, he fitted the bill (*Bentley*, 77). Blake's admirers were sufficiently impressed to pay for a collection of his juvenilia to be printed as a volume entitled *Poetical Sketches* in 1783, and something of their attitude towards Blake can be heard in the 'Advertisement' to the volume which explains:

> The following Sketches were the production of untutored youth, commenced in his twelfth, and occasionally resumed by the author till his twentieth year [. . .] Conscious of the irregularities and defects to be found in almost every page, his friends have still believed that they possessed a poetic originality, which merited some respite from oblivion. These their opinions remain, however, to be now reproved or confirmed by a less partial public. (*E*845)

Curiously, Blake himself seems to have been quite indifferent to the volume, and in 1784 would write a narrative in his Notebook entitled *An Island in the Moon*, which was, in part, a satire of the Mathew circle. In this extract, Blake depicts a flurry of characters talking nonsense in an attempt to parade knowledge on an array of subjects:

> In the Moon as Phebus stood over his oriental Gardening "O ay come I'll sing you a song" said the Cynic. "The trumpeter shit in his hat" said the Epicurean "& clapt it on his head" said the Pythagorean. "I'll begin again" said the Cynic
>
> Little Phebus came strutting in
> With his fat belly & his round chin
> What is it you would please to have
> Ho Ho
> I won't let it go at only so & so

> Mrs Gimblet looked as if they meant her. Tilly Lally laughed like a Cherry clapper. Aradobo asked "who was Phebus, Sir?". Obtuse Angle answerd, quickly, "He was the God of Physic, Painting, Perspective, Geometry, Geography, Astronomy, Cookery, Chymistry, Mechanics, Tactics, Pathology, Phraseology, Theology, Mythology, Astrology, Osteology, Somatology in short every art & science adorn'd him as beads round his neck." (p. 3, *E*450)

In the same year as he wrote *An Island in the Moon*, Blake set up a shop selling and making prints in partnership with James Parker, who had been a fellow apprentice with Basire. The venture, however, was short-lived, and the following year, 1785, Blake and Catherine left the shop and moved to a new home with Blake's younger brother Robert (*Bentley*, 97). The bond between the brothers was very close and, alongside Blake's ongoing commercial work, he taught Robert to engrave. There are some surviving pictures attributed to Robert, but only a few: around this time he contracted tuberculosis, and Blake nursed him up to the time of his death in 1787. Robert was 24, Blake, 29 at this time, and it was the most affecting bereavement of Blake's life.

At this point of his career, the intellectual and imagistic force of Blake's mature work had yet to appear. Although *Poetical Sketches* contains pieces discussing the tyranny of kings, it doesn't make the direct engagement with contemporary ideas which would characterize the works that followed. For in those works to come, Blake would not only tackle directly the revolutionary events of his day (as in *America: A Prophecy* or *The French Revolution*), but he would also engage with the philosophical and religious issues that were interwoven with them. As Blake recognized, intellectual, social and political histories cannot be separated out, and his poetic analysis of the revolutions that he lived through is therefore bound up with an analysis of the intellectual movement that informed those revolutions: the Enlightenment.

THE ENLIGHTENMENT

The term 'the Enlightenment' refers to a combination of changes in the way in which science, philosophy, politics and religion – among other things – were reconceptualized in Europe during the late-seventeenth and eighteenth centuries. In particular, the term signifies the rise and eventual pre-eminence of 'reason' in these different fields, grounded in a commitment to the idea that the universe is an ordered entity, and that its order could be understood through the use of reason (i.e. rational thought). This intellectual programme had significant social and political implications because one of the aspirations of Enlightenment thinkers was to use the light of reason to dispel the mystery and superstition under which, in their opinion, people had long lived and suffered. By making reason a new touchstone for understanding, Enlightenment thinkers were able to scrutinize and re-evaluate inherited attitudes towards previously unquestionable phenomena such as monarchy and religion. Thus the Enlightenment meant a new kind of scepticism, and a new willingness (and ability) to question ideas that had previously been beyond investigation.

This philosophical context provided the ideological impetus to the revolutions of the period because insofar as reason was independent of hierarchy or tradition, it could provide critical analysis of institutions that were rooted in those phenomena. Its consequent radical potential can be seen in Thomas Paine's critique of monarchy in *Common Sense* (1776). Paine (1737–1809) writes:

[There is a] distinction for which no truly natural or religious reason can be assigned, and that is, the distinction of men into KINGS and SUBJECTS. Male and female are the distinctions of nature, good and bad the distinctions of heaven; but how a race of men came into the world so exalted above the rest, and distinguished like some new species, is worth enquiring into, and whether they are the means of happiness or of misery to mankind. (Paine, 72)

The power of such writing lies in its openness and immediacy, but for political work like Paine's to have the impact it did, it needed not only to be written, but also to be communicated. Paine succeeded on both fronts as *Common Sense* was distributed as a pamphlet in America, selling over 100,000 copies, and as a result was a seminal influence on the revolution that followed. In Britain the connection between publishing and radicalism was also strong, but depended on the existence of publishers who were willing to take the risk of putting out radical material. One such individual, the publisher of Paine in England, was Joseph Johnson.

Joseph Johnson (1738–1809) was at the heart of radical intellectual life in London during the later eighteenth century, and it was Johnson that Blake was working for as an engraver from 1779 (*Bentley*, 108ff). In this capacity, Blake engraved plates for books including works by Mary Wollstonecraft, John Stedman and Erasmus Darwin. This work put him within reach of many of the major intellectuals of his day, although again his social standing here might have been similar to that in relation to the Mathew circle. Nonetheless, from working in this context, Blake recognized the possibility of entering public debate as an independent voice, and he began work on a piece entitled *The French Revolution* (1791), which he discussed with Johnson for publication. It is a work that shows Blake – now eight years on from the printing of *Poetical Sketches* – attempting to engage with the most important political event of his poetic maturity through 'prophetic' verse.

THE FRENCH REVOLUTION

The French Revolution was related to the American Revolution both ideologically and financially. Before the Revolution, France had an absolute monarchy, no taxation on the aristocracy, and a consequently precarious economic situation that had been exacerbated by French financial support of the American Revolution. The French Revolution took place in response to these socio-economic conditions, and was made possible by a reconceptualization of society drawing on Enlightenment thought that foregrounded new ideas about the value of human life and a commitment to 'freedom, equality and brotherhood' (*Liberté, égalité, fraternité*). In its early stages, the Revolution was largely peaceful but, as events progressed, the motivating ideals took an increasingly strong hold in the minds of some of its agents. Those leading the Revolution started to split into factions, some accusing others of not being revolutionary enough, tensions increased and violence broke out. Within a few years the king was beheaded, and thousands of French aristocrats, priests and prisoners were executed. By 1793 France was at war with England, and peace would not return to Europe for more than 20 years.

Blake's response to the French Revolution was mixed, not least because of his scepticism over the increasingly tyrannical ideology that accompanied it, and this is also true of his response to Enlightenment thought. Despite his admiration of figures such as Paine, his distrust of monarchy, Church and state, his loathing of Empire and oppressive traditions, and his non-conformist background, Blake had a complex and often antagonistic relation to Enlightenment ideas. In fact, Blake makes key Enlightenment thinkers, such as the French and Franco-Swiss philosophers Voltaire (1694–1778) and Jean-Jacques Rousseau (1712–78), into targets of his art (see, for example, his notebook poem 'Mock on Mock on Voltaire Rousseau', E476). Because of such attacks, Blake is sometimes described as an anti-Enlightenment figure, though this is a simplification, as his criticisms co-exist with sympathy for many aspects of Enlightenment thought. He never used the term 'Enlightenment' (it only began to be used retrospectively, well into the nineteenth century), but he certainly considered his own work to be responding to a contemporary ideological position, which he usually identifies as 'reason'. However, it is not so much reason itself that Blake objects to, as a particular use of reason.

BLAKE'S CRITIQUE OF REASON AND EMPIRICISM

What Blake disliked was the conjunction of empiricism (the belief that the only valid knowledge is that which can be derived from sense experience) with 'reason' (the logical interrelation of ideas premised on that empirical evidence). Reason, in Blake's view, has no content of its own, but is a way of interrelating knowledge, and can therefore only connect sense experience to other sense experience, producing what he calls 'a ratio of the five senses' (*Marriage*, pl. 5, *E*34). To claim – as some contemporary thinkers did – that this was the only acceptable form of knowledge represented, for Blake, a contraction of human experience, as it effectively disavowed inspiration, emotion, art, religion, and so on, as valid sources of understanding. Blake is not making a fine-tuned philosophical argument here, but is responding to the hegemonic (that is, culturally dominant) position of a certain combination of ideas at a particular historical moment. Reason is not something malevolent to be eschewed, but rather it is a key part of being human, and had been socially beneficial insofar as it allowed people to shake off the shackles of tradition and hierarchy. However, having attained ideological pre-eminence, reason began to legitimate only one form of experience, and therefore had come to represent a new form of tyranny.

For Blake, this type of thought had its origins in the work of three British thinkers: the philosopher Francis Bacon (1561–1626), the scientist Isaac Newton (1642–1727), and the empiricist philosopher John Locke (1632–1704). In brief, Bacon's advancement of experimental method anticipated the philosophical position of empiricism; Locke had brought this empirical methodology to psychology, arguing that there is no innate knowledge, and the mind can only know any thing through the senses; and Newton, using a combination of empirical investigation and reasoning, had provided an integrated account of the universe as a self-operating mechanistic system. In his later work, Blake used these three intellectuals to embody the tradition he felt he was responding to, grouping them together as an inverted Trinity, worshipping a debased, de-spiritualized form of the material world:

> Bacon, Newton, Locke,
> Deny a Conscience in Man & the Communion of Saints & Angels
> Contemning the Divine Vision & Fruition, Worshiping the Deus

Of the Heathen, The God of This World, & the Goddess Nature
Mystery Babylon the Great, The Druid Dragon & hidden Harlot
(*Jerusalem*, pl. 93, *E*253)

The apocalyptic language here is drawn from the Book of
Revelation, the last book of the Christian Bible, and is the sort of
imagery that Blake may have been familiar with from his Moravian
mother. In his later work, Blake would embody this conjunction of
reason and empiricism in a number of figures, pre-eminently in his
tyrannical creator-God Urizen (i.e. 'your reason') who will be discussed in Chapter 2. Blake's ready use of extreme biblical imagery
and his willingness to mythologize contemporary events brings into
focus the divergence between Blake and many of the key intellectual
figures of his day with regard to religion.

DEISM AND UNITARIANISM

The Enlightenment commitment to reason had not only entered
political and social thinking in the period, but inevitably it had also
entered religion. One of the most influential theological traditions
to develop during the eighteenth century was Deism. Deism was not
a religious denomination (although Blake can sometimes make it
sound like one) so much as an approach to the Creator that could be
found among different types of thinkers including both Anglicans
and dissenters. Historically, Deism has been typified as an intellectual tradition according to which God had created the universe but
then left it to its own operation without further intervention (a view
that could fit with Newton's mechanistic vision of the universe).
Whereas the Bible had traditionally been understood as revelation –
that is, as a form of knowledge that was not accessible by any other
means – it was now to be judged against the standards of 'reason'.
For Deists who continued to adhere to the Bible itself, this meant
disavowing those parts of scripture that did not accord with their
notion of reason – for example, Christ's miracles in the New
Testament. Famous Deists of the eighteenth century included
Thomas Paine, whom Blake had probably met (*Bentley*, 110ff),
Voltaire and Rousseau.

The tradition of Deism strongly influenced Unitarianism, a dis-
senting sect associated with many of the pre-eminent intellectuals of

Blake's day, including Joseph Johnson, the early feminist Mary
Wollstonecraft (1759–97), the chemist and philosopher Joseph
Priestley (1733–1804), the young Coleridge, and, for a period, the
political thinker and novelist William Godwin (1756–1836).
Unitarianism represented a serious attempt to strip religion of its
supernatural content, and to fuse Christianity with Enlightenment
rationality. As its name indicates, Unitarianism meant a rejection of
Trinitarianism (belief in a three-person God) in favour of belief in a
single God. This one God was a universal force, and was not the man
Jesus Christ. Christ was considered to be an enlightened teacher, but
only a man, and not God. It was here that Blake and the Johnson
circle parted ways, because while Blake may have had much in
common with the Deists and Unitarians on political grounds, his
religious position was very different. As noted above, Blake considered reason to be uncreative and only able to describe relations
between existing things, which made it inadequate in a religious
context. Blake was committed to an alternative religious perspective
whereby knowledge could be gained through what he would come to
call 'the Poetic Genius' or 'the Imagination', and he believed that
every individual has prophetic (that is, visionary, not fortune-telling)
abilities. This 'imaginative' response was fundamental to religion for
Blake because he saw Christianity as the radical attempt to bring
about a transformed world of social justice or, in other words, the
kingdom of God. Blake was not alone in his outlook, however, as he
is connected to those non-conformist traditions that claim their
authority through direct, individual experience of the divine that
supersedes the claims of the Church to mediate the individual's relationship with God. This type of religious energy, of confidence in a
personally and socially radical and transformative experience that
Blake connects to here, is known as 'enthusiasm'.

ENTHUSIASM, MILLENARIANISM, THE APOCALYPSE

The term 'enthusiasm' (from a Greek origin, meaning 'to be filled
with a god') is used to describe a type of religion that is rooted in a
personal and usually emotional (rather than 'rational') experience of
God. During the eighteenth century, it was visible in public forms of
religious experience, such as the emotionally dramatic conversions
at the field preaching of John Wesley (1703–91). Wesley himself was

speaking to the working classes, who had been effectively dropped from the remit of the Church of England, and for him to take their spirituality seriously was in itself politically radical. Enthusiasm came, as it were, from below rather than above, and it was perceived by those with power (cultural, social or political) as potentially dangerous. As Jon Mee writes:

> The fear of popular prophecy was heightened by contemporary theories of the psychopathology of enthusiasm. From Locke onwards enthusiasm had been presented as a contagious disease capable of rapidly infecting the lower orders. To many the Methodist revival seemed to be corroborating evidence of this weakness in the popular mind. (Mee, 49)

The treatment of enthusiasm as a dangerous infection bears a clear similarity to the treatment of Blake by some of his contemporaries as 'mad' (this will be discussed further in Chapter 4). One of the characteristics of enthusiasm and one of the reasons that it was perceived as a political threat is its ready use of apocalyptic imagery drawn from the Bible, the sort of imagery discussed earlier in relation to Blake's treatment of Bacon, Newton and Locke.

The Book of Revelation describes the apocalypse – the passing away (or violent destruction) of the present heaven and earth – and the creation of a new heaven and earth. This process involves an overthrowing of earthly powers (depicted as the Beast and the Whore of Babylon) and the subsequent establishment of God's kingdom. The book also describes a period of 1,000 years of peace on earth in which Satan (the Beast) is bound, and Christ rules on earth prior to Armageddon, the final battle of good and evil. The belief that this period of 1,000 years (the 'millennium') is about to begin, or has already begun on earth, is known as 'millenarianism'. During Blake's lifetime, many people believed that the French Revolution (at least in its early phases) signalled an overthrow of corrupt earthly powers and that this must signify the beginning of the millennium. A similar interpretation of the English Civil War had been made 150 years earlier, and many writers of the time saw explicit parallels between the situations of England in the 1640s and the 1790s. Millenarian claims required the ability to interpret contemporary political events in relation to the dense symbolic and numerological schemes of the Book of Revelation. Those who claimed the ability to do so announced themselves as prophets and there were plenty of them about at this time, particularly in London.

Blake, too, declared himself a prophet (this will be discussed in more detail below), and made extensive use of the language of apocalypse, but he does so in a characteristically ambiguous manner, deploying these ideas, and yet mocking them at the same time. In *The Marriage*, for example, he writes:

> The ancient tradition that the world will be consumed in fire at the end of six thousand years is true, as I have heard from Hell. (*Marriage*, pl. 15, *E*38)

The tone here, as throughout *The Marriage*, is playful, and this may have been partly self-defensive as *The Marriage* shows Blake distancing himself from the time in 1789 when he and his wife Catherine had attended and signed up to their one encounter with organized religion: the Swedenborgian New Jerusalem Church (see, for example, pl. 21, *E*41–2, and *Bentley*, 126ff). Emanuel Swedenborg (1688–1772) was a Swedish inventor and scientist who became, later in life, a religious writer. His works include *A Treatise Concerning Heaven and Hell*, which describes the author's discussions with angels, and *The Marriage* takes its title from – and is modelled in part on – this book. Blake was certainly strongly influenced by Swedenborg in his early career, but by the time of *The Marriage* had outgrown the latter's religious system, and was keen to demonstrate his independence from it.

Swedenborg is only one of the philosophers mentioned in *The Marriage*; Blake also shows his familiarity with alchemical and mystical writers, including Jacob Boehme (1575–1624), the shoemaking mystic from Görlitz, and Paracelsus (1493–1541), the astrologer and occultist from Switzerland. Blake's books from this period, one of his most productive, are full of this mix of apocalypticism, radicalism, enthusiasm, irony and ambiguity. They reflect the intense political, religious and social climate of London during this time.

Britain was divided in its response to the French Revolution. In the early part of the Revolution (1789–93) there was widespread support for events in France, particularly among intellectuals and artists, even though France had declared war on Britain in 1793. The anti- and pro-revolutionary positions can be seen respectively in Edmund Burke's *Reflections on the Revolution in France* (1790) and Paine's reply *The Rights of Man* (1791–2). However, after the execution of the King in 1793 and the beginning of the Reign of Terror later that year, the British government became acutely anxious that the Revolution would spread to England and result in similar turmoil and bloodshed. In addition to this was the anxiety that the French would invade Britain, which was certainly a possibility, and French troops did land in Wales in 1797. The government's response was the 'gagging acts', a number of separate pieces of legislation that aimed to control print publications and public meetings. As a result, Blake put himself in real danger from the government through his own radical writings at a time when the state was not only paranoid about the possibility of a revolution in England, but also actively, and often violently, trying to suppress any possibility of sedition.

In 1790 Blake and Catherine had moved to Lambeth, then a rural place, and they lived in relative prosperity in a large terraced house, even having enough money to employ a servant for a period (*Bentley*, 122–4). Blake's printing press was in the house, and he worked from there, close to the centre of political events and to the patriotic groundswell that now began to threaten radicals:

> The hysteria engendered by Tom Paine may on occasion have come close to Blake. The counter-revolutionary Society of Loyal Britons organized ritual protestations of loyalty all over the country, and on the night of 10 October 1793 they marched singing through the streets, threatening or even assaulting citizens who did not ostentatiously share their views, and burning effigies of Tom Paine. Blake may have seen the mob which met in Mount Row, Lambeth, very near his house in Hercules Buildings. (*Bentley*, 113)

Here, in Hercules Buildings, Blake produced the majority of his illuminated books including *The Songs of Innocence and of Experience* (1789–94), *The Marriage of Heaven and Hell* (1790–3), *America: A Prophecy* (1793), *Visions of the Daughters of Albion* (1793), *The First Book of Urizen* (1794) and *Europe: A Prophecy* (1794).

FELPHAM AND THE TRIAL FOR SEDITION

In 1800 Blake and Catherine, for the only time in their lives, left London to live elsewhere. They moved to Felpham, a small rural village on the south coast of England, to be near Blake's employer, William Hayley. Hayley (1745–1820) was himself a poet and biographer of sufficient renown to be offered the position of Poet Laureate in 1790. He was also wealthy, well connected and had a constant stream of projects in hand for which he wished to maintain Blake as a resident artist. Initially the Blakes were happy there, although the relationship between Blake and Hayley soured as Blake increasingly felt that his employer was using him as a tool and allowing him no imaginative exercise of his own. Hayley was keeping Blake employed, fed and housed, but was constricting his imaginative output. This seems to have been the source of Blake's comment 'Corporeal Friends are Spiritual Enemies', which had its origin in a letter discussing Hayley (*E*722). Gradually the Blakes' feelings about Felpham changed, but what really brought their stay there to an end was perhaps the most dramatic event of Blake's life, which took place in the summer of 1803.

France and Britain had revived their war at this time, and many British soldiers were stationed on the south coast. A regiment of dragoons had recently taken up residence in Blake's village of Felpham, and one of these soldiers, John Schofield, ended up in Blake's garden. Blake asked him to leave and, when Schofield refused, Blake took him by the arms and pushed him 50 metres down the street to the local inn where his fellow soldiers were quartered. Schofield was angry, possibly drunk, and almost certainly embarrassed by the event. In order to exact revenge, he accused Blake of sedition – that is, of damning the king and expressing his support of the French. The accusation was serious and Blake had to subsequently stand trial on the charge and, although he was ultimately acquitted, he had faced the possibility of a fine or imprisonment. The event seems to have had a profound effect on Blake and his art, as his work becomes more intensely personal after this time, and increasingly mythologizes events such as the encounter with Schofield. This is evident in *Milton* (1804–8), but much more so in the work that occupied Blake for the next 16 years: *Jerusalem: The Emanation of the Giant Albion* (1804–20).

The Blakes returned to London, close to where they had originally lived, and the city again assumed a central place in Blake's work. London is everywhere in his poetry, from the short lyric of that name in *Songs of Experience* to the reconfiguration of London as Jerusalem in his epic *Jerusalem*. Blake's treatment of England and London are complex, because they represent not only places for him, but power. Despite Britain's comparatively small size, it was a major power in the eighteenth century due to its technological, economic and naval strengths. Blake was, throughout his career, deeply opposed to Empire (as the title of David Erdman's famous book suggests, Blake conceived himself as a 'Prophet against Empire'). For Blake, Empire represented the power of the god of this world (Satan), it meant warfare, and it meant a society guided by the dictates of money. Blake could see the rise of Empire not only at home, but also across the channel in France, where the Revolution morphed into a new imperialism as France began to annex or occupy its neighbours. Napoleon rose to power during this period and crowned himself Emperor in 1804, and the subsequent Napoleonic wars continued until his defeat by Wellington at Waterloo in 1815. Thus for the greater part of Blake's writing career – from his mid-thirties until his late fifties – Britain was not only at war, but was also ruled by a government that was anxious to repress radicalism.

LATER LIFE

In terms of major life events, very little happened to Blake from this time until his death in 1827. He held a public exhibition in 1809 (which will be discussed in Chapter 4), but the majority of his time was consumed by seeking employment and executing commissions. Blake and Catherine had very little money, and lived accordingly. Blake was largely unknown to the public at this time, but he did develop important friendships, many of which were with artists such as John Linnell, who had sought Blake out and who wished both to learn from Blake and to help him if he could. The best-known of these artists is Samuel Palmer, who, along with a group of other young men who called themselves 'the Ancients', befriended Blake in his later years, spent time with him and celebrated his genius. Encouraged by such friendships, Blake continued to be artistically productive right to the end of his life, and many of his later works were commissioned by admirers like Linnell. Blake suffered no diminishment of artistic power as he aged, and some of his greatest works, such as his *Illustrations to the Book of Job*, were only completed shortly before he passed away. Blake and Catherine lived to the ages of 69 and 70 respectively (the younger Catherine outliving her husband by four years). The account of Blake's death came from Catherine herself and was recorded by one of the Ancients, Frederick Tatham, very shortly after Blake died. The account is so striking that it has recently been the subject of critical scrutiny, and it is clear that it is a literary artefact as much as a record of facts. Nonetheless, this description of events has a power of its own, and is the closest we have to a first-hand account of how Blake's life ended:

"Kate you have been a good Wife, I will draw your portrait." [said Blake] She sat near his Bed & he made a Drawing, which though not a likeness is finely touched & expressed.

He then threw that down, after having drawn for an hour & began to sing Hallelujahs & songs of joy & Triumph which Mrs Blake described as being truly sublime in music & in Verse. *He* sang loudly & with true extatic energy and seemed too happy that he had finished his course, that he had run his race, & that he was shortly to arrive at the Goal, to receive the prize of his high & eternal calling. . . . His bursts of gladness made the room peal again. The Walls rang & resounded with the beatific Symphony.

After having answered a few questions concerning his Wifes means of living after his decease, & after having spoken of the writer of this, as a likely person to become the manager of her affairs, his spirit departed like the sighing of a gentle breeze, & he slept in company with the mighty ancestors he had formerly depicted. (Tatham quoted in *Bentley*, 437)

STUDY QUESTIONS

1. Read 'The Sick Rose' in *Songs of Experience*. How do the themes and imagery here compare to those of 'I saw a chapel all of gold'?
2. Look at 'Nurse's Song' in *Innocence* and 'Nurses Song' in *Experience*.

What does Blake say in these two poems about the relationship between power, personal experience, memory, rule-making and the value of others' experience? Are there similarities between the nurse's relation to the children and that of a state to its citizens?

CHAPTER 2

LANGUAGE, STYLE AND FORM

What do Blake's books look like? Because he designed and printed his own works, each one is unique, and a copy of the *Songs* looks very different from a contemporary book printed in a standard format such as the first edition of Wordsworth and Coleridge's *Lyrical Ballads* (1798). *Lyrical Ballads* presents square-set black printed text on a slightly off-white page. By contrast, Blake's books are alive with colour and form, their pages bear the textures of his printing methods, the words not in typeface but in a hand-written script, between their lines the words growing into tendrils, human and animal forms, and other types of decoration; and standing amid the poetry are images of the naked human form, expressing anger, beauty and terror. Nothing else looks quite like Blake's books, though they are in a visual and literary dialogue with other forms of contemporary publication, such as the chapbook.

CHAPBOOKS AND PAMPHLETS

Chapbooks were small, cheaply printed pamphlets for the popular market, containing fairy stories, nursery rhymes, ballads and so on, and they were widely available in the eighteenth century. They represent (among other things) an early form of children's literature, an audience Blake was glad to reach: 'I am happy to find a Great Majority of Fellow Mortals who can Elucidate My Visions & Particularly they have been Elucidated by Children who have taken a greater delight in contemplating my Pictures than I even hoped' (*E*701). Mary Wollstonecraft and Hannah More were also writing works for children at this time, and Blake's *Songs* were probably influenced by Isaac Watts' *Divine Songs Attempted in Easy Language for the Use of Children* (1715). Blake also drew on popular forms of literature for adults, such as the pamphlet.

The pamphlet was a popular publication format in the eighteenth century because it was short, unbound, often without illustration, cheaply printed, and affordable at a time when books were expensive. Moreover, its ease of dissemination gave it real potential to effect change, as Paine's *Common Sense* had made evident during the American Revolution. It was consequently popular for political, philosophical and religious treatises of the period, and Blake can be seen drawing on this aspect of the pamphlet format and its characteristic numbered statements in the early works *All Religions are One* (*E*1–2) and *There is No Natural Religion* (*E*2–3). Here the format seems functional, but in *The Marriage*, for example, Blake subverts the model by laying out a series of propositions and counter-propositions as before, but simultaneously destabilizes our trust in the text by labelling them 'The Voice of the Devil' (pl. 4, *E*33). This ambiguous or subversive use of layout is carried through into Blake's use of the Bible. Bibles in Blake's day (as now) were often printed in double columns of text, and in *The First Book of Urizen*, which is Blake's rewriting of Genesis, Blake lays out his poetry in the same format. He also adopted the form of the biblical book of Proverbs for his 'Proverbs of Hell' in *The Marriage*. Blake's licence in rewriting the Bible came in part from his emulation of the most famous English poet to rework the Bible in a literary context, John Milton.

JOHN MILTON

Milton was perhaps the single most important author to influence Blake, and Blake, like many writers of the Romantic period, looked to Milton as a role model. Milton's significance lay not just in the scale and ambition of his art, but in the fact that he was as deeply involved in the revolutionary politics of his day as he was in writing. Milton had been Cromwell's Latin Secretary, had written documents against the king, had supported his execution, had supported the civil war, and was a religious non-conformist. His artistic, political and religious radicalism and greatness were of a piece, and this position as an inspired, bardic, political interventionist is exactly the role that many writers of the Romantic period aspired to. In Blake's case, however, this was not an unalloyed admiration. Blake was critical of Milton and disliked, for example, the latter's use of classical sources, which Blake considered to be a form of servitude (also found in Shakespeare) that was ruining art:

> Shakespeare & Milton were both curbed by the general malady & infection from the silly Greek & Latin slaves of the Sword.
> (Preface to *Milton*, E94)

Blake was not content with simple criticism, however; his prophetic work *Milton* is the story of how Blake redeems his predecessor by allowing him to pass through the regenerative medium of Blake's own body. It is a strange narrative to say the least, as can be seen from even a short excerpt: this is the moment when Milton – falling from the sky like Satan in *Paradise Lost* – first enters Blake's foot:

> Then first I saw him in the Zenith as a falling star,
> Descending perpendicular, swift as the swallow or swift;
> And on my left foot falling on the tarsus, entered there;
> But from my left foot a black cloud redounding spread over Europe.
> (pl. 15, E109)

As in the extract from *America* quoted earlier, Blake is again choosing mythological and epic modes through which to write his account of political, psychological or aesthetic revolutions.

In addition to his long poem about Milton, Blake produced numerous illustrations to Milton's poetry, including *Paradise Lost* and *Paradise Regained*. He shared clear epic aspirations with Milton, and the two poets also shared an interest in pastoral in their early careers: Milton had used the genre in *Lycidas* and Blake would do so in *The Book of Thel*.

PASTORAL

Pastoral is an ancient genre used by classical writers depicting idealized life in a rural context. In the hands of Romantic writers, such as Wordsworth, the traditional formal qualities of pastoral tend to disappear, but the preoccupation with nature (often in explicit contrast to the city) remains. Blake's use of the form is most evident in *The Book of Thel*, which employs pastoral motifs to narrate the symbolic story of a soul's encounter with experience. The book begins with these lines:

> The daughters of Mne Seraphim led round their sunny flocks.
> All but the youngest; she in paleness sought the secret air.
> To fade away like morning beauty from her mortal day:
> Down by the river of Adona her soft voice is heard:
> And thus her gentle lamentation falls like morning dew. (pl. 1, *E*2)

Pastoral often focuses, as here, on the life of shepherds, and, when it is used by Christian writers, this takes on a special meaning because it echoes biblical imagery in which God and Christ are depicted as shepherds (e.g. Psalm 23, John 10.11), and in which Christ is presented as the Lamb of God (e.g. John 1.36). The fusion of pastoral and Christian elements that Milton uses in *Lycidas* is also visible in some of the *Songs of Innocence*, including 'The Introduction', 'The Lamb', 'Night', 'Spring' and 'The Shepherd':

> How sweet is the Shepherds sweet lot,
> From the morn to the evening he strays:
> He shall follow his sheep all the day
> And his tongue shall be filled with praise.
>
> For he hears the lambs innocent call,
> And he hears the ewes tender reply,
> He is watchful while they are in peace,
> For they know when their Shepherd is nigh. (*E*6)

Blake is not interested in direct observation of natural phenomena, his lambs and ewes are symbols. This forms a striking contrast with the attention to natural scenes that can be found in a contemporary writer such as Coleridge. In 'This Lime Tree Bower my Prison' (1797), for example, Coleridge writes:

> Behold the dark green file of long lank weeds,
> That all at once (a most fantastic sight!)

Still nod and drip beneath the dripping edge
Of the blue clay-stone. (Coleridge, 138)

There is nothing like this kind of attentive natural description in Blake's poetry; his nature, whether pastoral or biblical, is invariably emblematic. This is the case even when Blake is depicting natural objects that are far from being pastoral. In *Songs of Experience*, poems such as 'The Sick Rose' and 'The Tyger' show something very different from the controlled, calm, organized reading of nature found in pastoral. The wild, threatening depictions of nature found in poems such as 'The Tyger' are much more clearly related to an important concept in the Romantic period called 'the sublime'.

THE SUBLIME

The sublime is not a genre so much as an aesthetic perspective found in different types of Romantic literature and art. Interest in the sublime had been increasing over the eighteenth century, particularly following the publication of Edmund Burke's *A Philosophical enquiry into the Origin of our Ideas of the Sublime and Beautiful* (1757). In this short work, Burke defined the sublime as anything characterized by obscurity, difficulty, magnificence, loudness, pain, power, terror, infinity, and so on. Traditionally these had been phenomena that people had sought to avoid. The novelty of Burke's work was his suggestion that this need not be the case, and that the sublime might, in fact, be a source of pleasure (as he puts it, 'pain can be a cause of Delight'). Burke develops his definition of the sublime by contrasting it (as his title suggests) with what he calls 'the beautiful':

> Sublime objects are vast in their dimensions, beautiful ones comparatively small; beauty should be smooth, and polished; the great [i.e. the sublime], rugged and negligent; [. . .] beauty should not be obscure; the great ought to be dark and gloomy; beauty should be light and delicate; the great ought to be solid, and even massive. They are indeed ideas of a very different nature, one being founded on pain, the other on pleasure. (Burke, 113)

The sorts of things that Burke claims produce the sublime include mountains and precipices, darkness, 'ghosts and goblins' (54) and 'the angry tones of wild beasts' (77). In short, the sublime corresponds to anything that exceeds or lies beyond the known or human capacity for understanding. The concept might be expressed in the words of one of Blake's 'Proverbs of Hell':

> The roaring of lions, the howling of wolves, the raging of the stormy sea, and the destructive sword. are portions of eternity too great for the eye of man. (*Marriage*, pl. 8, *E*35)

There was an important relationship between the sublime and religion during this period. The attributes of the sublime included unknowability and infinity, and these were qualities traditionally attributed to God. For those who had rejected the Church and were looking for an alternative place to encounter God, nature had a special appeal because its sublime qualities seemed to coincide with those of the divine. This is why so many of the poems, novels and paintings of the period depict experiences of striking natural scenery (often the Alps) in language that would usually be associated with religious experience. For example, in a major Gothic novel of the period, *The Mysteries of Udolpho* (1794), Ann Radcliffe writes:

> The road now descended into glens, confined by stupendous walls of rock, grey and barren, except where shrubs fringed their summits, or patches of meagre vegetation tinted their recesses, in which the wild goat was frequently browsing. And now, the way led to the lofty cliffs, from whence the landscape was seen extending in all its magnificence.
> [. . .]
> [T]he travellers had leisure to linger amid these solitudes, and to indulge the sublime reflections, which soften, while they elevate, the heart, and fill it with the certainty of a present God! (Radcliffe, 28)

Blake, however, is sceptical of the privileging of nature that this sort of outlook entails. He recognizes it as a central characteristic of Wordsworth's poetry, and writes accordingly:

> I see in Wordsworth the Natural Man rising up against the Spiritual Man Continually, & then he is No Poet but a Heathen

Philosopher at Enmity against all true Poetry or Inspiration
(*E*664)

Blake is out of step with his contemporaries here, and this is characteristic of his independence of thought and conception of design. He has little interest in nature as a source of the sublime, but is deeply interested in the sublime as a psychological and aesthetic category. It's a term that appears a good deal in his work, particularly in connection with his ideas of the imagination and eternity, and it is a key influence on the incorporation into his work of a contemporary style that foregrounded the sublime: the Gothic.

THE GOTHIC

During the eighteenth century, one of the central literary modes to evolve in relation to the discourse of the sublime was that of the Gothic. I call it a 'mode' rather than a 'genre' because is has no particular formal characteristics (in the way that a sonnet or an ode does), but is characterized by particular types of event or sensation. The Gothic dwells on feelings of psychological terror, physical horror, incarceration, disgust, obsession and superstition, and attempts to evoke these in its reader. Major Gothic texts contemporary with Blake's early major works include Matthew Lewis's *The Monk* (1796) and Radcliffe's *The Mysteries of Udolpho* which contains not only Gothic horrors, but lengthy descriptions of sublime Alpine scenery, such as the extract quoted above. Blake had no special interest in writing Gothic literature, nor did Wordsworth, yet both of their juvenilia contain examples of experiments in the mode (respectively, *Poetical Sketches* and *The Vale of Esthwaite*.) Blake's poem, 'Fair Elenor' in *Poetical Sketches*, is a notable example:

FAIR ELENOR
The bell struck one, and shook the silent tower;
The graves give up their dead: fair Elenor
Walk'd by the castle gate, and looked in.
A hollow groan ran thro' the dreary vaults.

She shriek'd aloud, and sunk upon the steps
On the cold stone her pale cheek. Sickly smells

Of death, issue as from a sepulchre,
And all is silent but the sighing vaults. (*E*410)

The castle, groans, shrieks, sickly smells and sighing vaults are all typical of Gothic. Blake lays aside this sort of ghost story in his later career, but the language, mood and imagery of Gothic continue to inform his mature works, such as *Urizen*:

Ages on ages rolld over them
Cut off from life & light frozen
Into horrible forms of deformity
Los suffer'd his fires to decay
Then he look'd back with anxious desire
But the space undivided by existence
Struck horror into his soul. (p. 13, *E*76)

The influence of Gothic is also visible in some of the images of torment that occur in Blake's later work, such as plate 25 of *Jerusalem*.

Within Gothic art and literature, religion is often treated not as a positive force but as an agent of cruelty, tyranny and torment. This treatment of religion is commonly effected by making its setting distant either in space, time or both, and for this reason many Gothic novels are set in Catholic monasteries or convents in continental Europe during the Middle Ages. Britain's own early religions, particularly druidism, offered a similar resource, and Blake, like many other writers of the period, portrays druidism as a savage, pre-Christian, naturalistic religion of sacrifice and bloodshed. In *Jerusalem* he describes how:

the Druids golden Knife,
Rioted in human gore,
In Offerings of Human Life (pl. 27, *E*171)

Wordsworth, in an early poem, is also threatened by druids and cries out, 'Why roull on me your glaring eyes | Why fix on me for sacrifice[?]' (*The Vale of Esthwaite*). It is no coincidence that both writers should be interested in this theme. During the eighteenth century, archaeology ('antiquarianism' as it was then known) had gained widespread interest, partly due to the work of William Stukeley, who had written about and speculated on the religious significance of Stonehenge and Avebury in the 1740s. This public interest also led to a number of literary forgeries of supposedly long-lost British myths. The best-known of these was the *Poems of Ossian*. Ossian was a figure from legend, an Irish poet and warrior, whose works were 'discovered' by James Macpherson, a Scottish poet, in the 1760s. In fact, they were not ancient, as Macpherson had forged them. Blake knew this, but nonetheless wrote about Macpherson (and Chatterton, another famous forger of verse):

I Believe both Macpherson & Chatterton, that what they say is Ancient, is so [. . .] I own myself an admirer of Ossian equally with any other Poet whatever (*E664–5*)

Although Blake does not attempt to pass off his own work as lost originals, he, like Macpherson, is trying to provide a mythology for the British Isles. Blake's most commonly read works, the *Songs* and *The Marriage*, are not mythological, but the majority of his works are: *Visions, Europe, America, Urizen, Milton, Jerusalem, The Four Zoas,* and so on, are all dense mythological narratives full of obscure and fantastic characters such as Los, Luvah, Tharmas and Urizen. Blake wrote his myths in the context of a society that was becoming increasingly interested in human origins and in discovering more about them through, for example, antiquarian studies such as Stukeley's. However, many intellectuals and artists of the day did not wish to locate their origins or inspiration in the imagined barbarity of prehistoric Britain, but preferred instead to ground themselves in the civilized, measured classical worlds of ancient Greece and Rome. If druidism represented one end of English culture, classicism represented the other.

CLASSICISM

'Classicism' refers to the opinion, common among European intellectuals and artists during the eighteenth century, that the height of human achievement had been attained in the classical world, which is to say in the arts and sciences of ancient Greece and Rome. Those who held this belief thought that these civilizations therefore provided the appropriate model for present-day European art and culture. Within literature, for example, classical works had been drawn on extensively by the generation of poets before Blake: Alexander Pope's translation of Homer's *Iliad* (1715–20) and *Odyssey* (1725–6), John Dryden's translations of Homer, Ovid and Virgil, and Milton's *Paradise Lost* are all examples. In the visual arts, classicism was enshrined in the Royal Academy, which privileged a style of art based on the study of classical models, and Blake himself had studied classical sculpture during his training there.

Blake admired many classical works, some of which (such as the Greek sculpture of the *Laocoön*) were sources of inspiration to him, yet he strongly objected to the cultural dominance of classicism in his own time. Blake identified classicism with an emphasis on rules, on traditions, on reason and order, and on mathematics and geometry. These emphases were visible, for example, in the symmetrical and geometrical forms of classical architecture. Classicism is oppressive for Blake because, like reason, it trades in a world of abstractions and ideals rather than in the particularities of human experience. Moreover (and for related reasons), Blake associates classicism with the celebration of war in Greek epics such as the *Iliad* and with, for example, the military imperialism of the Roman Empire. Intellectual servitude towards these cultures, Blake thinks, can only lead the Europe of his day into further conflict, a view which was perhaps justifiable given the contemporary creation and expansion of the French Empire, with the new Emperor Napoleon at its head. Blake writes:

> The Classics, it is the Classics! & not Goths nor Monks, that Desolate Europe with Wars. (*On Homers Poetry*, E269)

Blake made his stand against classicism by drawing on a very different aesthetic tradition which he had encountered through studying Gothic art and sculpture in Westminster Abbey. 'Gothic' in this context carries a different (though related) meaning to the eighteenth-century 'Gothic' discussed above. It refers to the art and architecture of the late-thirteenth to early sixteenth centuries, and is most strikingly embodied in the cathedrals of the period. Blake contrasted the 'Mathematic Form' of the Greek world-view to the 'Living Form [that is] is Eternal Existence' of Gothic (*E*269).

Blake's view of how classicism subjugates the particulars of human life to generalizations and abstractions can be helpfully illustrated by John Ruskin's differentiation of Greek from Gothic architecture in 'The Nature of Gothic'. Ruskin argues that in Greek architecture, all parts of the building are subordinate to laws and geometrical principles that govern the whole design. In Gothic architecture, by contrast, each part of the design has its own life: spires sprout gargoyles, pillars become intricately and individually carved, in each detail individual workmanship is expressed, just as it is in the complex, decorative forms of Blake's own printed books. For Ruskin, this uniformity or variation in style corresponded directly to the way in which human beings are treated:

> Wherever the workman is utterly enslaved, the parts of the building must of course be absolutely like each other; for the perfection of his execution can only be reached by exercising him in doing one thing, and giving him nothing else to do. The degree in which the workman is degraded may be thus known at a glance, by observing whether the several parts of the building are similar or not; and if, as in Greek work, all the capitals are alike, and all the mouldings unvaried, then the degradation is complete; [. . .] if, as in Gothic work, there is perpetual change both in design and execution, the workman must have been altogether set free. (Ruskin, 93)

Although Ruskin was writing after Blake, this is a helpful perspective from which to understand Blake's view of classicism, in which he saw individual 'genius' being sacrificed in favour of higher, abstract principles. For both Blake and Ruskin this connects to the 'degradation' and enslavement of human individuals, and for both writers, aesthetic and religious beliefs are inseparably interconnected.

CLASSICISM, THE BIBLE, AND SOCIAL ORDER

The cultural dominance of classicism in Blake's day had deep social implications because the language of classicism was the language of Empire. Classicism represented the architecture, painting and literary style favoured by the court, and, moreover, it was the language of the grammar school and the university, as study at Oxford and Cambridge were grounded in a knowledge of Greek and Latin. It required privilege, money and training to be able to speak the language (in its widest sense) of classicism, and it was not therefore democratic. This is another reason why the Bible was a political resource for Blake: comparatively few households would have been familiar with works of classical literature, but almost every home would have had a copy of the Bible. Blake was consequently deeply invested in the idea that the Bible was universally accessible, so when Dr Johnson wrote:

> The BIBLE is the most difficult book in the world to comprehend, nor can it be understood at all by the unlearned, except through the aid of CRITICAL and EXPLANATORY notes (*E*666)

Blake responded:

> Christ & his Apostles were Illiterate Men. Caiphas, Pilate & Herod were Learned. The Beauty of the Bible is that the most Ignorant & Simple Minds Understand it Best. (*E*666)

There is an important cultural and religious history behind this dispute which is connected to the discussion of the Reformation given in Chapter 1. Before the Reformation – and despite certain medieval attempts to the contrary – interpretation of the Bible had been the jurisdiction of the Church. The Bible had not been immediately accessible to the laity – first, because many people couldn't read; second, because the Church used Latin translations of the Bible which few could understand; and third, because before the invention of printing, Bibles were inconceivable as personal possessions except for the very wealthy. A number of social and technological developments concurrent with the Reformation changed this, including the translation of the Bible into the vernacular (i.e. English), and the spread of printing. This allowed the possibility of personal interpretation of the Bible, which coincided powerfully with the concept of personal divine inspiration emphasized by religious enthusiasm.

Blake saw the Bible as a complex fragmented text, at odds with classical norms of order and decorum, and he was not alone in this.

Throughout the seventeenth and eighteenth centuries, writers had been puzzled by the Bible because, although it represented the word of God, it did not seem to match up to the artistic excellence of classical literature. This perceived inequality was because of a lack of understanding of the organizational principles of Hebrew literature. This began to change, however, in 1753 when Bishop Robert Lowth delivered his *Lectures on the Sacred Poetry of the Hebrews*. Lowth's lectures showed that although Hebrew poetry did not conform to the compositional rules of classical literature, it did have a coherent prosody of its own (Roston, 23). Not only did this mean that the Bible could be understood and appreciated as a work of art in its own right, but it also meant that those who wrote the Hebrew Bible – including prophets such as Isaiah and Ezekiel – could be understood not just as prophets, but as poets too. Writers such as Blake extended this logic by suggesting that if the biblical prophets had been poets, poets could therefore be prophets. This begins to make some sense of why he called a number of his works 'prophecies', why he adopted and adapted biblical forms in his writing, and why he felt a strong sense of shared identity with those whom he considered to be his biblical predecessors.

This new poetic model of Hebrew poetry did not conform to the decorous norms of classical art; it was visionary and individualistic with an emphasis on personal prophetic inspiration which enabled Blake to claim that his own works were inspired by the same muse – the Holy Spirit – that had inspired the Bible itself. Not everyone agreed with Blake's perspective, however, and rather than foregrounding the radical disparity of this alien Hebrew literature, some writers wished to reincorporate it into the conservative norms of classicism. The conflict between the two positions is amusingly illustrated by Blake's response in the last year of his life to a new translation of the Lord's Prayer (Matthew 6.9–13). The translation from the Greek had been made by Dr Robert Thornton, who had previously employed Blake to illustrate, among other things, his edition of Virgil's Pastorals. Thornton sought to translate the Lord's Prayer into what he considered to be suitably decorous language, and came up with the following:

O Father of Mankind, Thou, who dwellest in the highest of the Heavens, Reverenc'd be Thy Name. May Thy Reign be, every where, proclaim'd so that Thy Will may be done upon the Earth as it is in the Mansions of Heaven. Grant unto me, and the whole world, day by day, an abundant supply of spiritual and corporeal food. Forgive us our transgressions against Thee, as we extend our Kindness, and Forgiveness, to All. O God! Abandon us not, when surrounded, by Trials. But preserve us from the Dominion of Satan: For Thine only, is the Sovereignty, the Power, and the Glory, throughout Eternity!!! Amen. (*E*668)

Blake was appalled by this translation and responded:

I look upon this as a Most Malignant & Artful attack upon the Kingdom of Jesus by the Classical Learned thro the Instrumentality of Dr Thornton. The Greek & Roman Classics is the Antichrist [. . .] This is Saying the Lords Prayer Backwards which they say Raises the Devil (*E*668)

Blake considers Thornton's pious, didactic translation of the prayer to be a thin veil for the author's underlying conservative, monarchist, materialist impulses, and Blake demonstrates this with unrestrained satire by 'translating' Thornton's translation back into 'vulgar English':

Doctor Thorntons Tory Translation Translated out of its disguise in the Classical & Scotch language into the vulgar English
     Our Father Augustus Caesar who art in these thy Substantial Astronomical Telescopic Heavens, Holiness to thy Name or Title & reverence to thy Shadow. Thy Kingship come upon Earth first & thence in Heaven. Give us day by day our Real, Taxed, Substantial, Money-bought Bread, [and] deliver [us] from the Holy Ghost (so we call Nature) [and from] whatever cannot be Taxed, for all is debts & Taxes between Caesar & us & one another. Lead us not to read the Bible but let our Bible be Virgil & Shakespeare, & deliver us from Poverty in Jesus that Evil one. For thine is the Kingship or Allegoric Godship, & the Power or War & the Glory or Law, Ages after Ages in thy Descendents. [F]or God is only an Allegory of Kings & nothing Else. Amen (*E*668)

Throughout his career Blake remained engaged in a battle to wrestle the Bible out of the hands of conservative forces, and in doing so he was often biting about how the language of self-satisfied elitism had made Christianity conspire with market economics and empire. Chapter 3 will consider in more detail how Blake thought these processes operated, and what philosophical and artistic strategies he offered in response.

STUDY QUESTIONS

1. There is no single term that can describe the genre of *The Marriage*. It is made up of a range of different genres, and the variety here is matched by the tonal variety of the work. Look through *The Marriage*, one section at a time, and consider what genre each section utilizes or reminds you of, and think about how it reads in different voices. How does the meaning alter if it is read as serious, as ambiguous, as tongue-in-cheek, as fantastic or as factual?
2. Look at 'Infant Joy', 'The Blossom', and 'The Shepherd' in *Songs of Innocence*. Who is the speaker in each of these poems? Are these poems *for* children, or do they attempt to represent the voices *of* children? If the latter, what challenge do they offer to us as adult readers? What part do language and form play in communicating this?

CHAPTER 3

READING BLAKE

Most readers first encounter Blake's poetry through the *Songs of Innocence and of Experience*. The two sets of poems are based on culturally familiar categories whereby 'innocence' and 'experience' stand in a linear relationship to each other. Traditionally, individuals are thought to move, chronologically, from the state of innocence to the state of experience, as in the change from childhood to adulthood. Conventionally, one state replaces the other, and the two cannot be concurrent. Blake's challenge to this paradigm is evident in the subtitle of the combined edition of the *Songs* which reads 'Shewing the Two Contrary States of the Human Soul'. In different editions of the *Songs* he shifts poems between categories because, in Blake's view, contrary states exist not in linear sequence, but in parallel: they are simultaneous.

This dynamic relationship between contraries is one of the structuring themes of Blake's art. His art is, in other words, dialectical, and one of his key insights is that individuals and groups within society gain power by attempting to shut down dialectic by relating one half of any paired opposite to 'good' and the other half to 'evil'. This is clear in the case of innocence and experience, whereby the former has been associated with purity and goodness, and the latter with a falling away into sin. This theme is not immediately obvious from reading the *Songs* because the nature of the relationship between the paired contraries of innocence and experience is not explicitly discussed in that work. It is easier to see in *The Marriage*, in which paired opposites and their moral labels are discussed at length. For example, *The Marriage* provides an extended discussion of the paired contraries of 'reason' and 'energy', two forces that correspond approximately to the 'conservative' and 'radical' forces that exist within an individual or society. The 'conservative' is the force that wishes to keep things the same; the 'radical' is the force that wants to change things. Conservatism benefits those who hold power (because if things stay the same, they will be able to maintain it); radicalism benefits those without power (because change gives them an opportunity to gain it). *The Marriage* provides a series of set pieces in which reason and energy are set up against each other, and the relationship between the two is illustrated or dramatized.

On plate four, for example, Blake sets out the polarity of the two forces in the form of a short philosophical tract as follows:

> All Bibles or sacred codes have been the causes of the following Errors.
> 1. That Man has two real existing principles Viz: a Body & a Soul.
> 2. That Energy, called 'Evil' is alone from the Body, & that Reason, called 'Good' is alone from the Soul.

By 'alone from the body' Blake means 'comes only from the body'. He then sets out the counterarguments to these positions:

> But the following Contraries to these are True
> 1. Man has no Body distinct from his Soul for that called Body is a portion of Soul discerned by the five Senses, the chief inlets of Soul in this age
> 2. Energy is the only life and is from the Body, and Reason is the bound or outward circumference of Energy. (pl. 4, *E*33)

Two different positions are set out here, and it might seem that the former 'errors' derived from 'Bibles or sacred codes' are simply to be replaced by Blake's new contraries. However, as noted earlier, this section is entitled 'The Voice of the Devil', so are we really meant to trust these assertions? *The Marriage* is full of this sort of shifting ground, whereby Blake engages us as readers to judge matters for ourselves. The 'Proverbs of Hell' provide one of the best-known examples: these represent 'infernal' wisdom, but there can be no simple or single response to them, as they are, by turns, witty, irreverent, serious, satirical, outrageous and tender. Blake uses similar strategies in his prophetic works, in which this central polarity of reason/energy (conservative/radical) is explored at greater length. In *The First Book of Urizen*, Blake embodies these forces in the characters of Urizen himself (reason) and Los (energy/creativity), two figures who become locked in a struggle of mutual definition.[1]

The Book of Urizen

Blake wrote *Urizen* shortly after completing *The Marriage* and *Songs of Experience*. The book is, among other things, a rewriting of the opening section of Genesis, the first book of the Bible. It tells the story of a God figure – Urizen – who exists in an uncreated dynamic universe. Urizen finds the constant flux of this universe intolerable, and responds – like a true conservative – by attempting to freeze the dynamic processes of being itself. He proclaims his rationale in these words:

> From the depths of dark solitude. From
> The eternal abode in my holiness,
> Hidden set apart in my stern counsels
> Reserv'd for the days of futurity,
> I have sought for a joy without pain, [. . .]
> For a solid without fluctuation (pl. 4, *E*70)

In the narrative, Urizen attempts to control the flux of the universe by subordinating the particulars of life to a set of increasingly complex laws and ideals – in other words, to abstract thought. This subjection of particulars to universal abstracts is the same process that Blake sees at work in classicism (as discussed earlier). One way of reading *Urizen*, therefore, is as a dramatization of the control processes at work in those who celebrate classical art, empirical rationalism or Enlightenment thought above all other modes of life. In Blake's dramatization, Urizen's attempt to deny flux amounts to a pathological process of division with no end-point, going ever deeper into a limitless void of abstraction. It is like a void of depression, where each negative thought multiplies itself, and deepens the depression still further. The awfulness of this process is recognized in the narrative by the other central figure of the book, Los. Los, the artist figure, the embodiment of energetic creativity, decides to limit

Urizen's self-inflicted horrors through a creative act. Urizen, who here represents the infinite regression of abstract thought, has, appropriately, no material form. Los limits his suffering by giving Urizen a body (up until this point Urizen has himself been an abstraction). Consequently, much of the narrative of *Urizen* is concerned with the creation of the body of its central character. This is an unusual narrative, and initially makes the book confusing to read. It is, however, easier to grapple with the story of Los and Urizen when it is related back to the relationship of energy and reason discussed in *The Marriage*. There, the dynamic relationship between the two is stated in these terms:

> Energy is the only life and is from the Body and Reason is the bound or outward circumference of Energy. (pl. 4, *E*33)

In other words, reason and energy, the conservative and the radical impulses, are two sides of the same coin, the form and content of the same reality. In *The Marriage* it is reason that controls energy (as the 'bound' or outward circumference of energy), whereas in *Urizen* it is Los (energy) who limits Urizen (reason). This reciprocity is important because it shows that either figure can occupy the restraining role.

The interdependence of opposites

The insight that Blake offers through these narratives is that what initially appear to be alternatives are fundamentally interdependent. Los and Urizen are not interchangeable opposites, they are necessary contraries, and this is true of innocence and experience, reason and energy, and all the other contraries that structure our existence. The essential thing to grasp about these contraries is that they are not alternative modes of life, but are necessary, in their duality, to human life: dark and light, innocence and experience, heaven and hell, tall and short, buyer and seller, and so on. Even if these are only 'conceptual' realities, we cannot think without concepts, their oppositions are necessary to existence. Contraries cannot be united, because to unite them would be to collapse existence itself (uniting day and night, dark and light, earth and water, would be to undo the world), as Blake writes in *The Marriage* of another set of contraries – this time of 'producers' and 'devourers' (loosely corresponding to radicals and conservatives):

> These two classes of men are always upon earth, & they should
> be enemies; whoever tries to reconcile them seeks to destroy exis-
> tence. Religion is an endeavour to reconcile the two. (pl. 16–17,
> E39)

'Religion', here, is the kind of religion that Urizen wants, a collapse
of experience into a single law, a single life, a single vision. How,
then, does this Urizenic form of religion come about?

One of the major themes of Blake's work is the depiction and
analysis of what happens when an individual or society makes a con-
certed effort to split contraries apart, to valorize one side and negate
the other. Urizen's downward spin into an abyss of abstraction and
his attempt to shut out energy depict the destructive nature of this
process. The issue is central to Blake because he thinks that the
process of splitting contraries apart is the basis of tyranny and social
injustice, and his work is motivated by the attempt to improve social
and individual life.

Blake's critique would be a straightforward matter if this process
of moral splitting were easily visible and could be dismissed as
simple megalomania or malevolence. The complication, and pathos,
come from the fact that this splitting is invariably done for the very
best reasons. So, in *Urizen*, Urizen's struggle is motivated by his
highest ideals, which he describes in terms that might be a summary
of the laws given in the Bible. Urizen seeks to establish:

> Laws of peace, of love, of unity:
> Of pity, compassion, forgiveness. (pl. 4, *E*71)

The problem is that because life and the universe are chaotic, in
order to achieve his benevolent goals, Urizen has to exercise a tyrannical rule over everything he encounters in order to make it conform
to his abstract system. His actions are intended to be liberating, but
his methods are incarcerating. As a result, however well intentioned
Urizen's motivations may be, what they turn into, in practice, is a
form of tyranny, because what he aspires to is:

> One command, one joy, one desire,
> One curse, one weight, one measure
> One King, one God, one Law. (pl. 4, *E*71)

To enact his vision, Urizen must, as this passage indicates, legislate all aspects of being. Urizen embodies that impulse that Blake identifies in classicism, in rational empiricism, and in conservative forms of religion, to control through law-making the energetic sources of life, particularly desire. The critique of this process is widespread in Blake's writings, and is articulated in a poem such as 'The Garden of Love' in *Songs of Experience*:

> I went to the Garden of Love,
> And saw what I never had seen:
> A Chapel was built in the midst,
> Where I used to play on the green.
> [. . .]
> And Priests in black gowns, were walking their rounds,
> And binding with briars, my joys & desires. (*E*25)

Here love is portrayed as a joyful, innocent freedom that is bound and suppressed with the thorny briars of institutional religion: the process of regulation is cruel and barbed.

In *Urizen*, Urizen becomes dangerous and causes suffering to himself and to others not because of some implicit negative quality of reason (which he represents), but because he attempts to use, gain or exert power, and to shut himself off from other aspects of experience. The story could easily be the other way round, and sometimes in Blake's mythology it is: without Urizen, uncontrolled energy erupts in the figure of Orc – the son of Los – the revolutionary who wants to smash and overturn everything: Orc is the spirit of revolution. The subtlety of Blake's work is that although Urizen is a tyrant, this does not simply make Urizen 'bad' and Los 'good'. Urizen is necessary to existence because energy becomes a destructive force without reason. To dismiss Urizen as 'bad' would be to engage in the very act that Blake is attempting to critique.

Contraries distinct from negations
Blake's point is that we solve nothing but only cause suffering by trying to negate one half of a contrary. Our aim should be to bring the two halves of any aspect of existence back into relationship, which is why he writes books with titles such as *Songs of Innocence and of Experience*, and *The Marriage of Heaven and Hell*. This does

not mean neutralizing the nature of contraries, rather it does mean recognizing their respective characters and differences without needing to attach moral labels to them. Blake clarifies this central tenet of his thought by distinguishing a 'contrary' from a 'negation'. Contraries are necessary to the existence of the world, but individuals and societies use contraries as a way to split the world in two morally. This moral splitting and categorizing is what Blake calls 'negation'. Negation is the process whereby one half of a pair of contraries is labelled as inferior to the other half and consequently dismissed. A government that crushes political dissent, silences opposition and imprisons or executes its critics is engaged in the attempt to negate experience. A negation is a zero-value or devalued contrary, which for Blake does not actually exist, because it is an abstract image of the world that no longer corresponds to reality itself:

Negations are not Contraries: Contraries mutually Exist:
But Negations Exist Not (*Jerusalem*, pl. 17, *E*161)

This is the process that Urizen attempts as he tries to shut out the flux of energy, dismissing it as 'bad', and seeking only after the order that he considers to be the 'good'.

The attraction of seeing the world in terms of 'good' and 'evil' is that it divides it up into a readily comprehensible moral scheme. Polarizing the world allows us to make moral judgements of it, and to act with confidence on those judgements. It is easier to act in a black-and-white world than in a world of shades of grey; in the face of definite good or evil than in situations that seem morally equivocal. Blake recognizes the social power of attaching moral schemes to contraries, and he analyses this process in *The Marriage*. Here he shows how religious conservatives attach the moral categories of 'good' and 'evil' to the necessary contraries of 'reason' and 'energy':

From these contraries spring what the religious call Good & Evil. [In their opinion,] Good is the passive that obeys Reason. Evil is the active springing from Energy. Good is Heaven. Evil is Hell (pl. 3, *E*33)

Here Blake is arguing that both reason and energy are necessary and interdependent, but that the 'religious' try to split them apart, confusing them for 'good' and 'evil'. In other words, the conservative powers that govern Blake's society call reason 'good' (because it maintains their own interests in the status quo) and energy 'evil' (as it threatens revolution, upset and change). Like Urizen, these conservative powers wish to devalue energy and to valorize reason. But for the radical who dwells within the same social structure, the moral labels would be reversed. The possibility of this reversal can be illustrated by the example of two soldiers telling the story of a war in which one soldier has fought for one side, and one soldier for the other. Each will tell approximately the same story of the war (in terms of key events, battles, chronology, and so on) but, where the one says 'good' the other will say 'evil', where one says 'evil' the other will say 'good'.

This process of moral labelling was central to the debate over the French Revolution. Supporters of the Revolution (such as Paine) saw the events in France as something good, the transformation of a corrupt society into an egalitarian one. Opponents (such as Burke) considered them to be bad: the destruction of value and tradition, a descent into chaos and strife. Blake dramatizes these polarized viewpoints in a passage in *The Marriage*, in which the narrator and his companion (an angel) look across the sea to France, where the Revolution is taking place. The conservative angel is frightened at the prospect of the Revolution spreading to England, and sees only an apocalyptic vision of terror. The imagery here is metaphorical and biblical: rather than a literal depiction of guillotines and mobs, the angel sees a black sun, a sea monster (Leviathan), clouds of smoke and fire. This vision, significantly, comes out from between 'black & white spiders' – perhaps representing polarized thoughts spinning webs of abstraction:

> But now, from between the black & white spiders a cloud and fire burst and rolled thro the deep blackning all beneath, so that the nether deep grew black as a sea & rolled with a terrible noise: beneath us was nothing now to be seen but a black tempest, till looking east between the clouds & the waves, we saw a cataract of blood mixed with fire and not many stones throw from us appeard and sunk again the scaly fold of a monstrous serpent. at last to the east, distant about three degrees appeard a fiery crest above the waves slowly it reared like a ridge of golden rocks till we dis-

coverd two globes of crimson fire. from which the sea fled away in clouds of smoke, and now we saw, it was the head of Leviathan. his forehead was divided into streaks of green & purple like those on a tygers forehead: soon we saw his mouth & red gills hang just above the raging foam tinging the black deep with beams of blood, advancing toward us with all the fury of a spiritual existence. (pl. 18–19, E40)

Horrified by this vision, the angel leaves the scene but, as he does so, his perspective on the Revolution goes with him, and the narrator, remaining behind, is then left to see the same scene in very different terms:

My friend the Angel climb'd up from his station into the mill; I remain'd alone, & then this appearance was no more, but I found myself sitting on a pleasant bank beside a river by moon light hearing a harper who sung to the harp. & his theme was, The man who never alters his opinion is like standing water, & breeds reptiles of the mind. But I arose, and sought for the mill, & there I found my Angel, who surprised asked me, how I escaped?

I answered. All that we saw was owing to your metaphysics: for when you ran away, I found myself on a bank by moonlight hearing a harper (pl. 19–20, E40–1)

The black shining sun has become moonlight; the raging foam of the black deep, a river; the monstrous sea serpent, a 'reptile of the mind'. Everything is the same, but its interpretation has changed completely. Throughout *The Marriage*, Blake shows the ways in which the same narrative can be told from contrary moral perspectives, demonstrating that the moral interpretation of narratives can never be fixed, but is forever open to negotiation.

Blake's reading of Paradise Lost

Blake's most famous example of this struggle to fix the moral meaning of narratives is his reading of Milton's 1667 epic *Paradise Lost*. Blake's infamous claim is that the hero of *Paradise Lost*, the saviour figure, is not Christ, but Satan: Blake argues that Milton's Satan is actually the Messiah. *Paradise Lost* deals with God and Devil, good and evil, heaven and hell, and Blake is able to make his argument by emphasizing the symmetry of the poem's moral scheme and by turning the tables on the narrative by telling the story from the point of view of the devils rather than the angels:

> [I]n *Paradise Lost* [. . .] Reason is called 'Messiah'. And the original Archangel or possessor of the command of the heavenly host, is called 'the Devil' or 'Satan' and his children are called 'Sin' & 'Death'. But in the Book of Job, Milton's Messiah is called 'Satan'. For this history has been adopted by both parties. (pl. 5, *E*33–4)

In the Book of Job (to which I will return), Satan acts on behalf of God as an accuser and prosecutor of Job, and Blake interprets Satan's role as that of a functionary of the law – that is, of reason. In *Paradise Lost*, however, the prosecuting agent is Christ, who is also acting on behalf of God. Blake's point is that the same role – that of urizenic moral prosecutor – is occupied by, or labelled, 'Christ' in one story, and 'Satan' in the other.

In Blake's view, Milton is a genius, who, as a poet, has a total grasp of the warring contraries that structure our existence. As a man, however, Blake thinks Milton was in some ways deeply conservative, and therefore misunderstood the moral significance of his own narrative. As Blake explains:

> The reason Milton wrote in fetters when he wrote of Angels & God, and at liberty when of Devils & Hell, is because he was a true Poet and of the Devils party without knowing it. (pl. 5, *E*34)

Blake is being playful here, and the point of his argument is not that he wishes to replace the conventional reading of *Paradise Lost* with a new orthodoxy, but rather that he wants to show that the story can be read in two different ways, and that the direction we read it in will depend on the preconceptions that we bring to the text as readers.

Blake shows that our moral interpretations are actually incidental to the genius of the work: *Paradise Lost* succeeds as poetry both for those readers who see Satan as the hero, and for those who see Christ as the hero. This is consistent with the unsettling fact that although the categories of 'good' and 'evil' persist across history and different cultures, their significance is unstable: one age's 'evil' can be another age's 'good'; one culture's 'good' can be another culture's 'evil'. This might seem to lead to an inevitable position of moral scepticism or relativism, but this is not Blake's goal. His caution regarding categorical moral thinking is not moral relativism, but a willingness to question whether we have necessarily always got it right. Blake's work asks, Why is that we can get it so very wrong, and why is it that even when we are wrong, we can still think we are right? Blake uses a range of different subversive strategies to unseat his reader's complacent – though well-meaning – moral categorizations of the world.

The central subversive strategy of *The Marriage* is that it sits heavily in favour of the joys of energy. This is because Blake thinks his own age is in the grip of reason, so he is overstating the case for energy to re-establish a dialectical relationship between the two – that is, to bring the contraries back into balance. Blake lives in a culture where the powers that be deem reason 'good', and energy (as in, say, political radicalism or religious enthusiasm) 'evil'. The joke of *The Marriage* (and the book is meant to be, among other things, funny) is that Blake accepts the use of conventional moral labels, and then simply swaps them around. He surprises the reader by taking sides with the devils against the angels, recording the 'Proverbs of Hell', and enthusiastically discussing the excitement and genius of the place. What of the angels? In Blake's narrative they are the conservative forces within society who understand themselves to be morally superior beings and have taken the name of the 'good' upon themselves. They are those who hold power in the government and the Church, which is why those who threaten the status quo – radicals – must play the part of devils.

The example of war

Within *The Marriage*, the angels represent what Blake considers to be the historically problematic combination of social power and moral authority. It is no coincidence that Blake's politically subversive text has a religious framework, because if an individual or state claims they are enacting the will of God, they have engaged the ultimate moral imperative. The clearest example of the power of this combination is the use of 'God' to authorize war. War is a practical activity – the deployment of troops, the use of firepower and so on – but to be carried out effectively it also needs to maintain an overarching moral narrative (such as having 'God on our side'). In a situation of war, the acts of an army will be constituted of thousands of individuals in tens of thousands of actions and encounters. The war could not proceed efficiently if the moral quality of each of these encounters had to be debated. If you believe you are fighting on the side of an overall good, it is not necessary to stop and question whether each and every act within that war is good or evil.

Blake recognizes that for something like a war effort to work, it is necessary to maintain a very wide focus and to overlook the details in order to preserve a generalized idea of 'good' that will prevail even in the face of the proliferation of particular evils, such as the torture of prisoners, friendly-fire casualties, and the bombing of civilians. For example, if a child is killed by a weapon, we may call this 'evil', but if we pan right out and see this as 'collateral damage' in a 'war for freedom' then we may be able to superimpose the label 'good'. Your team is the good team, your country is the good country, you are committed to those thematic ways of thinking that require subordinating details to the principle. This, remember, is also what Blake considered to be the goal of classicism: subordination of individual parts to the greater concept.

In summary, in Blake's view, moral categorizations of the world invariably become bound up with power issues and particularly with generalizations – 'abstractions', as Blake calls them – that subordinate the particulars of individual existence. Blake is committed to the idea that our experience of the universe is made possible by phenomena having contrary qualities (such as darkness and light, reason and energy); however, he opposes the attachment of moral labels to these qualities for three reasons:

1. It is philosophically erroneous to suppose you can do away with one half of existence (by labelling it as 'bad').
2. The desire to do so is invariably a cloaked attempt to gain or maintain power over others, although this may not be clear to the perpetrators, who will be doing it for 'the best reasons' (i.e. the 'good').
3. The prioritization of moral schemes leads to generalizations that overlook the particulars of human existence.

The following section will look at (3) – that is, the collapsing of the rich diversity of human experience into what Blake calls 'single vision', and the role that narrative has in this process.

PART TWO: THE ROLE OF NARRATIVE

And this is the manner of the Sons of Albion in their strength
They take the Two Contraries which are calld Qualities, with which
Every Substance is clothed, they name them Good & Evil
From them they make an Abstract, which is a Negation
Not only of the Substance from which it is derived
A murderer of its own Body: but also a murderer
Of every Divine Member: it is the Reasoning Power
An Abstract objecting power, that Negatives every thing
This is the Spectre of Man: the Holy Reasoning Power
And in its Holiness is closed the Abomination of Desolation
(*Jerusalem*, pl. 10, *E*151–2)

The passage describes how the perceptions of an individual or a society are based on the contraries with which 'every substance' (i.e. phenomenal reality) is clothed, and how those individuals or societies attach moral qualities to contraries, and from these create an abstract scheme of reality which, Blake argues, is a negation of reality itself. It is a negation because it is a mental abstraction that replaces reality. This abstract scheme invariably presents itself as an idea of 'absolute truth' that underpins reality: whether that truth is scientific, political, economic, religious or something else. One example would be when 'religion' looks at innocence and experience, calls one 'good' and the other 'bad', replaces engagement with the realities of these aspects of life with an abstract moral scheme, authenticates it by linking it to God, and then uses its own institutional power to punish the things it has labelled as 'bad'. Another example would be an empirical form of science, in which objectivity is valorized, while emotion, subjectivity, and so on, are denigrated. The goal here would be an abstract model of the universe in which the human component is removed and where laws of physics and atoms interact in a remote world of abstraction. In each of these cases, an abstract scheme is read as that which underlies all other realities. The model can be seen at work in present-day religious fundamentalists who want religion to explain science (hence, for example, Creationism), and in secular thinkers who want science to explain religion (hence, for example, Social Darwinism).

Abstraction: the source of tyranny

One of Blake's key insights is to show that such quests, whatever goods they produce, can also be the source of power, tyranny and inhumanity. Blake thinks that the problem arises because these abstract schemes seem to exist beyond space and time, and therefore no longer need to take account of the particular situation of individuals: these abstractions put themselves 'above' or 'beyond' the human, beyond the contingencies of individual lives. Historically, the conjunction of such schemes with military or state power has led to bloodshed: religious wars, wars fought over nationhood, wars fought over ideas such as 'freedom', extermination in the name of 'racial purity', capital punishment for the protection of 'society', and so on.

Blake's art is centrally concerned with suffering and injustice, and therefore an analysis of the function of abstraction is at the heart of his work. Blake has three particular things to draw out in relation to this topic. First, ideological narratives are general not particular: in attempting to get to an objectivity beyond the human, these narratives have no truck with particularities. Newton wasn't interested in which apple fell on his head (was it a Golden Delicious or a Granny Smith?); he was only interested in the 'reality' *behind* it – that is, the question of what governs *any* apple, or *any* planet. Blake calls this type of thinking 'abstract', because abstract means 'dissociated from any specific instance'. He sees the same thought process at work in the sort of moral logic that says: Never mind who the individual is, or what their circumstances are, is euthanasia itself good or evil? Second, all abstractions and knowledge structures are embodied as narratives. There is no escape from narrative because all abstractions depend on ordered explanations of the nature of things. Cosmology, capitalism, geometry and theology are all narratives. It is no way out to say that they are only a way of communicating a reality that lies beyond them: as the whole enterprise of modernism and postmodernism has shown (whether in the work of Joyce, Woolf, McCluhan, Derrida, Foucault or a host of others), narratives are not, and can never be, transparent media; they create – or at least modify – the reality that they explain. Third, all narratives are human. There is no way of removing the human component and seeing from a non-human perspective. It requires a human to create or describe any abstract scheme, though the scheme itself may well not acknowledge this dependency (often describing itself as 'objective').

Abstraction is always non-human in Blake; human life always exists in what Blake calls 'minute particulars'. This is one of the most important conflicts in his work, and the refusal to subjugate the human perspective to 'higher' schemes is a hallmark of his art. The subjugation of the human by the abstract, and its social and individual impact, is the subject of the two 'Chimney Sweeper' poems of *Songs of Innocence and of Experience.*

The 'Chimney Sweeper' poems

Songs of Innocence and of Experience are closely engaged with the life of the marginalized. The poems are not spoken by the hegemony (society's rulers) – none of the speakers are churchmen or politicians or capitalists – instead the speakers are the marginalized: women (such as the nurse), infants and children. And those poems that are not spoken by the marginalized are about them, such as the hapless soldiers and prostitutes in 'London'. Right at the bottom of the social heap of eighteenth-century London were child chimney sweeps. Children were used for this job, of course, because they were small enough to be forced up chimneys to clean them and remove blockages and, moreover, they had few, if any, legal rights:

> Blake would have known that an attempt was made in 1788 to improve the conditions of child chimney-sweeps: eight was the proposed minimum age; hours of work would be limited; regulations were proposed to ensure that sweeps were properly washed every week; and a ban proposed on the use of children in chimneys on fire. In the event, the Porter's Act was not passed. (Wu, 63*n*)

It is one such child that becomes the narrator of 'The Chimney Sweeper' in *Experience*:

> A little black thing among the snow:
> Crying weep, weep, in notes of woe!
> Where are thy father & mother? say?
> They are both gone up to the church to pray.
>
> Because I was happy upon the heath,
> And smil'd among the winter's snow:

They clothed me in the clothes of death,
And taught me to sing the notes of woe.

And because I am happy, & dance & sing,
They think they have done me no injury:
And are gone to praise God & his Priest & King
Who make up a heaven of our misery. (*E*21–2)

The child is weeping in the snow when the narrator of the opening
lines encounters him (see Blake's accompanying image). Surprisingly, the child is not an orphan, he has parents, but the parents are
the cause of his suffering, or at least they allow it to continue while
they are at church ('gone to praise God & his Priest & King'). The
parents have not gone to church because they are evil people, but
because, presumably, they believe it is the right thing to do. The
question that Blake brings into focus here is: How is it that the
pursuit of an abstract good (represented by church-going here) can
lead to particular evils (in this case, child neglect)? The poem
shows that exploitation exists because a system of ideas (here,
religious 'good') is being put before the welfare of the child. In
other words, an abstract idea of good has been given precedence
over the miseries of a particular human life. For such reasons,
Blake is not interested in the idea of doing 'good' in the abstract,
and he writes:

> He who would do good to another, must do it in Minute Particulars
> General Good is the plea of the scoundrel hypocrite & flatterer
> (*Jerusalem*, pl. 55, *E*204)

In the *Experience* poem, the child realizes what's going on and is
sufficiently astute to depict (his parents' understanding of) God,
Priest and King as a power alliance, a trinity making up 'a heaven of
our misery'. In this respect the *Experience* poem is fairly straightforward: the child is neglected and narrates the reasons for his neglect.
But Blake has a companion poem in *Innocence* also entitled 'The
Chimney Sweeper' that goes a step further:

> When my mother died I was very young,
> And my father sold me while yet my tongue,

Could scarcely cry weep weep weep weep.
So your chimneys I sweep & in soot I sleep,

Theres little Tom Dacre, who cried when his head
That curl'd like a lambs back, was shav'd, so I said.
Hush Tom never mind it, for when your head's bare,
You know that the soot cannot spoil your white hair.

And so he was quiet, & that very night,
As Tom was a sleeping he had such a sight,
That thousands of sweepers Dick, Joe, Ned & Jack
Were all of them lock'd up in coffins of black,

And by came an Angel who had a bright key,
And he open'd the coffins & set them all free.
Then down a green plain leaping laughing they run
And wash in a river and shine in the Sun.

Then naked & white, all their bags left behind,
They rise upon clouds, and sport in the wind.
And the Angel told Tom if he'd be a good boy,
He'd have God for his father & never want joy.

And so Tom awoke and we rose in the dark
And got with our bags & our brushes to work.
Tho' the morning was cold, Tom was happy & warm,
So if all do their duty, they need not fear harm.

The poem is similar to that in *Experience* in that it is a narrative told
by a child chimney sweep. The child relates his effective orphaning,
and the hard life that such children live, in which their only solace
and solidarity lie in each other. This is followed by the dream section
of the poem, in which the children are liberated by an angel. It's a
religious image, baptismal, showing a wonderful scene of emancipation, but it is also dark and full of pathos, because the implication is
that this release is actually death. After this vision, the children
return to work nourished and supported by both the dream and the
words of the 'angel', but these words are sinister and full of threat
as the subtext of the last line is 'If you don't do your duty, you'd

better fear harm'. The angel, as in *The Marriage*, appears to be a representative of power, perhaps the children's employer, who is using the language of religion to enjoin them to accept their miserable fate. The key way in which this story differs from that of the *Experience* poem is that the child – and herein lies his 'innocence' – has swallowed and internalized the narrative that keeps him enslaved. Like the parents in the *Experience* poem, he cannot properly see his own suffering because it is obscured by the promise of a higher 'good'. This disempowers the child because he cannot change his situation unless he can first see it. At least the *Experience* child may have some chance of improving his situation, if he doesn't die of neglect first.

The two poems are acute in their social analysis, and show that Blake is not simply interested in pointing his finger at the tyrants in society, as he recognizes that the issues are more complicated than that. It is tempting to put blame on the parents in the *Experience* poem, but should blame be placed on the child in the *Innocence* poem for effectively doing the same thing? Everyone involved is subject to the destructive systems that they perpetuate; even the 'innocent' child internalizes them. Nonetheless, there are guilty parties here: just because a narrative or system of power is ingested by everyone does not mean that it is not therefore benefiting *someone*. Blake sees clearly how the powers that be within any culture – the hegemony – invariably have self-authenticating abstract narratives.

God as human projection

If what the parents in 'The Chimney Sweep' worship – like the angels in *The Marriage* – is an abstraction that perpetuates tyranny and neglect, where then does Blake stand on religion? After all, given that God is supposed to be infinite, eternal and in every way 'above' humanity, doesn't that make him the ultimate abstraction? Blake agrees that it does, and argues that this *is* the God of many people: a God who can be invoked for war, patriotism, oppression, and judgement of others. Yet Blake doesn't think this to be the true God. In common with later figures such as the philosophers Ludwig Feuerbach (1804–72) and Karl Marx (1818–83), Blake considers this abstract God to be a human projection of our own punitive and legalistic selves.

Throughout history, Blake thinks, people have (mistakenly) identified this projection with Jehovah. This projected 'God' is the scourge of Blake's work, and he appears in many forms: Urizen is one of them, though Blake sometimes (humorously) calls him 'Nobodaddy' (that is, 'nobody's daddy'). He is an alarming figure, visible in many of Blake's pictures and poems that present a cruel, blind, malevolent God. This is, however, a God that Blake rejects. In an insightful and moving fictional representation of Blake entitled *In Lambeth*, Jack Shepherd gives Blake these lines:

> God isn't *up there* you know, sitting in judgment, as it were, on a cloud, with a long white beard, inventing awful rules so that people feel guilty all the time, and so on . . . That's someone else entirely. [. . .] Many people worship this horrible emanation and call it God. A *good* God and a *just* one. . . . They're wrong of course. For if this *good* God were in fact *just*, as they suppose, the world he created would be *just* too. But the world *isn't* just. Society isn't just! Far from it . . . (Shepherd, 11)

This is the God, Blake thinks, whom people use as an excuse in war, and Blake satirizes the image of the God that he thinks people are worshipping. In a poem about the French Revolution, for example, he writes:

Then old Nobodaddy aloft
Farted & belchd & coughd
And said I love hanging & drawing & quartering
Every bit as well as war & slaughtering

Then he swore a great & solemn Oath
To kill the people I am loth
But If they rebel they must go to hell
They shall have a Priest & a passing bell (Blake's Notebook, E498)

The worship of this false God leads to unnecessary suffering. The suffering comes about because this 'God' sets up iron rules that no human being can keep, and then blights them with plagues for their failure to do so, while tormenting them psychologically at the same time with the threat of hell. Blake thinks that this God – a tyrant who tortures those in his power – cannot be distinguished from what people have traditionally called 'the devil'.

One of Blake's most powerful depictions of this God is in his illustrated interpretation of the Book of Job. Very briefly, the traditional interpretation of the Job story is that Job is a rich and righteous man. God decides to test his righteousness by sending Satan to torment him to see if he will renounce God. Job's life is ruined but, though he questions God, he ultimately remains faithful and is eventually restored to even greater wealth than he had at the outset of the story. Blake's interpretation is rather different. He thinks that at the beginning of the story, Job is worshipping the false God discussed above: Job's 'God' is a projection of Job's own idea of righteousness, which is to say, Job is effectively worshipping an idealized self-image. Job's sufferings begin because of his inability to live up to this idealized self-projection, and he undergoes the most intense psychological suffering as a result. Below is Blake's illustration of Job 7.14, 'thou scarest me with dreams, and terrifiest me through visions':

In the picture, Job lies on his bed, with 'God' hovering over him, pointing to the Ten Commandments with one hand, and to hell with the other. The message is clear: Be morally perfect or be damned. Job is in terror because he knows (as a human) that he cannot be perfect, and this 'God', therefore, has become his persecutor and tormentor. It is for this reason that Blake depicts Job's God with horns, a cloven hoof, and as being bound round with a serpent. Under this intolerable pressure, Job, of course, cracks. Job's restitution ultimately comes when he relinquishes this self-projection, and is thereby open to an encounter with the true God.

If this isn't God, then, who or what is Blake's God? And why is Blake preoccupied with the Bible (which he calls 'the Great Code of Art') if he thinks that for many people God is an imaginary tyrant who causes real world destruction?

PART THREE: JESUS

To answer these questions, it is necessary to discuss Blake's reading of the Gospels, and his understanding of Jesus. In Blake's view, there is a great discrepancy between the abstract God and the human Jesus. He writes:

> Thinking as I do that the Creator of this World is a very Cruel Being & being a Worshipper of Christ I cannot help saying "the Son O how unlike the Father." First God Almighty comes with a Thump on the Head Then Jesus Christ comes with a balm to heal it. (*E*564)

Law and prophecy

Blake correlates this difference between the abstract God and Jesus with two different biblical traditions: that of law and that of prophecy. 'The Law' and 'the Prophets' describe two of the principal sections of the Hebrew Bible (the 'Old Testament'). For Blake, law and prophecy stand in a similar relationship to each other as reason and energy. In the Bible, 'Law' relates to the prescriptions for human conduct, which have divine endorsement and regulate and define what is acceptable in the sight of God, whereas 'prophecy' is either about prediction ('foretelling') or speaking on behalf of God ('forth telling'), in which the prophet uses imaginative and perhaps symbolic means to illuminate or criticize human conduct. Both are concerned with human behaviour, but Law addresses the issue through regulation, prophecy through inspiration, and particularly the exercise of imagination.

In a discussion at the end of *The Marriage*, the narrator argues explicitly that Jesus is guided by prophetic impulse and not by the Law:

> [N]ow hear how [Jesus] has given his sanction to the law of ten commandments: did he not mock at the sabbath, and so mock the

sabbaths God? murder those who were murderd because of him? turn away the law from the woman taken in adultery? steal the labor of others to support him? bear false witness when he omitted making a defence before Pilate? covet when he pray'd for his disciples, and when he bid them shake off the dust of their feet against such as refused to lodge them? I tell you, no virtue can exist without breaking these ten commandments: Jesus was all virtue, and acted from impulse: not from rules. (pl. 23–4, *E*42)

Jesus here is not a slave to rules, but an energetic and imaginative interpreter of them. This passage foregrounds Blake's perennial theme that Christianity is not about simply following laws or moral codes (both of which are abstract), because if that was what constituted Christianity, it would be no different from moral philosophy. As Blake puts it, 'If Morality was Christianity Socrates was the Saviour' (*Laocoön*, *E*274).

Prophecy constitutes an act of interpretation rather than a statement of rules, and Jesus does not, in Blake's opinion, bring a new set of laws into operation so much as a new focus on interpretation, and new ways of engaging with the Law. This can be seen in the many debates and conflicts that Jesus enters into in the Gospels over the interpretation of the Law. Typically, there is a disagreement between Jesus and the religious authorities about how the Law should be interpreted. Jesus repeatedly challenges the way in which the religious authorities have used the Law. Jewish Law is detailed and complex, but Jesus says that its function can be summarized as serving two purposes: love of God and love of neighbour. Thus, when asked, 'Which is the greatest commandment in the Law?', Jesus replies:

'Love the Lord your God with all your heart and with all your soul and with all your mind.' This is the first and greatest commandment. And the second is like it: 'Love your neighbour as yourself.' All the Law and the Prophets hang on these two commandments. (Matthew 22.35–40)

How, then, is love of God to be expressed? The nature of the relationship between these two commandments may be clarified a few chapters later in Matthew's Gospel when Jesus suggests that love of God might be expressed through love of one's neighbour. The scene is the day of judgement, and God (the King) has just reminded the righteous of how in the past they have fed, clothed and cared for him. The righteous have no memory of such an encounter with God and are puzzled by this:

> Then the righteous will answer him, 'Lord, when did we see you hungry and feed you, or thirsty and give you something to drink? When did we see you a stranger and invite you in, or needing clothes and clothe you? When did we see you sick or in prison and go to visit you?' The King will reply, 'I tell you the truth, whatever you did for one of the least of these brothers of mine, you did for me.' (Matthew 25.37–40)

Here the act of love towards God and the act of love towards a fellow human are one and the same thing, and the former takes place through the latter.

This identification of divine love with human love is a common theme in Blake, and is evident, for example, in his poem 'The Divine Image' from *Songs of Innocence*:

> To Mercy Pity Peace and Love,
> All pray in their distress:
> And to these virtues of delight
> Return their thankfulness.

> For Mercy Pity Peace and Love,
> Is God our father dear:
> And Mercy Pity Peace and Love,
> Is Man his child and care.

> For Mercy has a human heart
> Pity, a human face:
> And Love, the human form divine,
> And Peace, the human dress.

> Then every man of every clime,
> That prays in his distress,
> Prays to the human form divine
> Love Mercy Pity Peace.

And all must love the human form,
In heathen, turk or jew.
Where Mercy, Love & Pity dwell,
There God is dwelling too (*E*11–12)

In Blake's view, we are called upon to engage with others (whether 'heathen, turk or jew', or beggar, sweep, prostitute, sinner or tax collector) as humans, and not to treat each other as symbols or functions of an abstract legal or moral code (for example, by one another them as 'sinners').

Love as humanization

In these terms, love is an act of imagination, whereby abstract or legalistic responses to individuals are humanized in the light of compassion (for example, by treating people as human individuals, not as statistics or stereotypes). This conflict of compassion and legalism is evident in Jesus' repeated encounters which pit his interpretation of the Law against that of the religious authorities. The religious authorities want a strict, literal application of the Law, whereas Jesus is committed to interpreting the Law through 'love' – that is, by foregrounding the human aspect of the situation (usually the suffering of an individual). Examples include Jesus healing a man with a shrivelled hand on the Sabbath (Matt. 12.10), allowing his hungry disciples to pluck corn on the Sabbath (Matt. 12.1–8), and refusing to condemn the woman caught in adultery (John 8.1–11). In each case, Jesus' act brings the suffering of an individual (the 'human' concern) into conflict with the Law. If love is the point of the Law (Matt. 22.36–40), then it would be absurd to make the Law conflict with compassion. Those who make the Law abstract are making it work against its own aims; in Paul's terms, they are guided by the letter rather than the spirit of the Law (Romans 7.6, 2 Corinthians 3.6); in Blake's terms, they are Urizenic tyrants, angels of hypocrisy.

To summarize this part of the discussion: Without love the Law is an abstraction and the beginning of tyranny. Divine love is encountered through human love, and human love prioritizes compassion over abstraction. Jesus is the fullest revelation of God that we can know as humans, because he is God in human form: 'God is Jesus' (as Blake writes in the *Laocoön*).

The Body of Christ

So far this book has focused largely on how Blake critiques religion, but his work does not all take this negative form; he also provides a positive articulation of his understanding of God. Blake's understanding of Jesus is drawn, in part, from the writings of St Paul. In Blake's view, if we love each other, we are brought into relationship and together constitute a larger body rather than being simply a conglomerate of self-centred individuals. Blake calls that larger body 'the Divine Body', which is his name for what Paul calls 'the Body of Christ'. In his letter to the Corinthians, Paul argues that together individual Christians participate in, and in fact compose, the Body of Christ:

> The body is a unit, though it is made up of many parts; and though all its parts are many, they form one body. So it is with Christ. [. . .] Now the body is not made up of one part but of many. [. . .] If they were all one part, where would the body be? As it is, there are many parts, but one body. The eye cannot say to the hand, 'I don't need you!' And the head cannot say to the feet, 'I don't need you!' [. . .] If one part suffers, every part suffers with it; if one part is honoured, every part rejoices with it. Now you are the Body of Christ, and each one of you is a part of it. (1 Corinthians 12.12–27)

Blake's use of this passage does not restrict its meaning to refer only to those who are members of the Church, or even to Christians; it is open to all people, as Blake argues it is through love that the eternal relation of all things is seen.

The image allows Blake, like Paul, to emphasize both the importance of individuality and the importance of community. From Paul, Blake takes another idea: Paul discusses what he calls 'gifts of the spirit' – wisdom, knowledge, faith, prophecy, and so on – and suggests that just as each person is an individual, so each person has a different gift, and it is through the exercise of these spiritual gifts that individuals participate in the Body of Christ. In Blake's terms, spiritual gifts are artistic gifts. I will say more about Blake's idea of 'art' below, but mention briefly here that it corresponds roughly to 'prophecy' as discussed above: art is the imaginative act which allows compassion to once again be prioritized over abstraction, and to bring humans back in relationship with each other and with God. Art is a mechanism, a temporal imaginative act that restores humans to this eternal perspective on their social unity, and it is only (as I will show below) incidentally related to activities such as writing, painting, or playing an instrument. The Body of Christ and the Imagination are synonymous in Blake's work. As with Christ, the Imagination is the point where the human and the divine meet. Blake writes in the *Laocoön*, 'The Eternal Body of Man is the Imagination, that is, God himself, The Divine Body, Jesus: we are his members' (*E*272). In Blake's theology, the Imagination is not something that individuals utilize or possess, but something in which they may participate.

Eternal truth, temporal error

Blake's ideas are rooted in traditions of thought going back at least to Plato that truth is eternal, and error is a temporal obscuration of truth. In this view, the world that we inhabit is a temporal, material, 'vegetable' world that reflects the eternal world like a mirror (or, as Blake calls it, a 'glass'). To understand the world in its eternal perspective, it is necessary, according to Blake, to see things in the context of the Body of Christ, which effectively means seeing the interconnectedness and holiness of all things.

> [The] world of Imagination is the World of Eternity[,] it is the Divine bosom into which we shall all go after the death of the Vegetated body[.] This World of Imagination is Infinite & Eternal whereas the world of Generation or Vegetation is Finite & Temporal[.] There Exist in that Eternal World the Permanent Realities of Every Thing which we see are reflected in this Vegetable Glass of Nature[.] All Things are comprehended in their Eternal Forms in the Divine body of the Saviour[,] the True Vine of Eternity[,] The Human Imagination (*Descriptions of the Last Judgment*, *E*555)

The limits of empiricism

This returns us to Blake's dissatisfaction with empiricism. The empirical position, by limiting knowledge to the senses, explicitly refuses to comprehend reality in the context of this larger, humanized, compassionate perspective. Blake depicts the empiricist position as one in which the unredeemed senses are shrunken inlets of light in a prison house of material being. He writes, 'man has closed himself up, till he sees all things thro' narrow chinks of his cavern' (*The Marriage*, pl. 14, *E*38). The 'cavern' here is the head and Blake envisages the individual as being enclosed in his or her own body such that eternity can only enter through 'narrow chinks': the eyes, ears, mouth and nose. Under empiricism, the senses become 'Five windows [that] light the cavern'd Man' (*Europe*, pl. iii, *E*59). In this state of shrunken perception the only part of the soul that an individual can recognize is that which can be registered with the senses, and that portion of the soul is, Blake says, the body. Hence he writes in *The Marriage*:

> Man has no Body distinct from his Soul for that calld Body is a portion of Soul discernd by the five Senses. the chief inlets of Soul in this age (pl. 4, *E*33)

The Marriage prompts consideration of the restraints of this empiricist vision by asking questions such as:

> How do you know but ev'ry Bird that cuts the airy way, Is an immense world of delight, clos'd by your senses five? (pl. 7, *E*34)

Throughout *The Marriage*, and elsewhere in his work, Blake calls for an expansion of the senses, to open them to this 'immense world of delight'. His argument is that to see reality, our sensory perceptions have to be combined with compassion or love, which means, effectively, that we need to see the world and each other with the eyes of God. It is then that the world will be seen in its eternal perspective. This is the context of Blake's famous stanza:

> To see a World in a Grain of Sand
> And a Heaven in a Wild Flower
> Hold Infinity in the palm of your hand
> And Eternity in an hour (*Auguries of Innocence*, *E*489)

Here the world of space and time have been put aside, and things are understood in their relation to the divine and the eternal, rather than simply to the time-bound ratio of the five senses dictated by empiricism. According to Blake, we effectively have choices in how we perceive the world, and it will appear entirely differently according to the choices we make:

I know that This World Is a World of Imagination & Vision[.] I see Every thing I paint In This World, but Every body does not see alike. To the Eyes of a Miser a Guinea is more beautiful than the Sun & a bag worn with the use of Money has more beautiful proportions than a Vine filled with Grapes. The tree which moves some to tears of joy is in the Eyes of others only a Green thing that stands in the way. Some See Nature all Ridicule & Deformity & by these I shall not regulate my proportions (*E*701)

For Blake, nature, the created world, is in itself neither good nor bad (either term would return us to the realm of negations). Nonetheless, it can be seen in error or in truth. If the world is engaged with exclusively empirically, it becomes a trap for the senses. If the world is understood as a part, or reflection of eternity, it offers access to the divine. Blake lived in a society in which the empirical view of the universe was gaining ground, and this caused him occasionally to lose patience with the natural world, in a most un-Romantic fashion that can border on contempt: 'I assert for My self that I do not behold the Outward Creation & that to me it is hindrance & not Action[:] it is as the Dirt upon my feet [–] No part of Me' (*Last Judgment*, *E*565).

Blake's myth *Urizen* narrates the creation of this restricted, empiricist world. In this work, nature is not the marvellous handiwork of a benevolent deity, but a tormented contraction of the Infinite, forged by Los as an act of compassion to limit Urizen's suffering. This is the universe that empiricism has brought into existence, the '*outward* creation' that Blake disavows.

Blake has a name for the state of being in which the individual regards materiality – the empirical universe – as the only reality: he calls it 'Satan', and characterizes it as 'the State of Death, & not a *Human* existence' (*Jerusalem*, pl. 49, *E*198, my italics). Participation in Satan is the opposite of participation in Christ, but this is not a dualistic scheme, as Satan is not the contrary, but the negation of Christ, the vacuum when all sight of Christ is lost. Satan is the supreme example of the 'negations' discussed earlier in this chapter. In the state of Satan, blind to eternity, individuals are possessed by their own selfhoods, and they form, in the agglomerate, not a transfigured Divine Body, but a horrible, non-human 'Polypus of Death' (*Jerusalem*, pl. 49, *E*336): 'By Invisible hatreds adjoind, they seem remote and separate | From each other; and yet are a Mighty Polypus in the Deep!' (*Jerusalem*, pl. 66, *E*218). Blake's image of the polypus is that of a jellyfish, a blob with no defining lines, no minute particulars; neither animal nor plant (so people believed), it functions symbolically as matter without form, a shapeless mass of 'living fibres'. This conglomerate of selfhoods is the anti-Christ, 'One Great Satan | Inslav[']d to the most powerful Selfhood: to murder the Divine Humanity' (*Jerusalem*, pl. 49, *E*197). Pure capitalism would be an example of the polypus, a system in which market value is prioritized entirely over human value, and in which individuals treat each other, and the world, as objects for consumption, as insignificant or worthless things, as just so many statistics. Redemption, in Blake's work, is a deliverance from this 'vast Polypus', the 'self-devouring monstrous human Death' of materialism (*Milton*, pl. 34) through reintegration into the Body of Christ.

Restoration to truth

For Blake, Jesus' life and teachings show how individuals can be liberated from states of error and restored to truth. Jesus encounters many individuals – such as lepers and prostitutes – who believe that they are worthless (and unclean) in the sight of God. Jesus redeems them by restoring them to a state of wholeness, of love, of self-worth, and of reconnection with God: in Blake's terms, he restores them to eternity. At the centre of Jesus' ministry and fundamental to this process is the forgiveness of sins. Throughout his work, Blake argues that the forgiveness of sins is *the* defining feature of Christianity, claiming 'This alone is the Gospel & this is the Life & Immortality brought to light by Jesus' (*E*875). Forgiveness is the willingness to release an individual into humanity again, by no longer binding them to the state of error through which they have passed: no longer reducing an individual life to an abstract label such as 'criminal', 'enemy' or 'outcast'. Thus in *Jerusalem*, one of the characters urges others to learn to 'distinguish the Eternal Human [. . .] from those States or Worlds in which the Spirit travels: | This is the only means to Forgiveness of Enemies' (pl. 49, *E*198).

Art equated with forgiveness

It is on this point that art is connected to Christianity for Blake. For Blake, art is a mechanism whereby this process of forgiveness, redemption and humanization can be brought about, specifically because art is capable of changing our perceptions ('cleansing the doors of perception', as Blake puts it in *The Marriage*). It is art (of which the Bible, for Blake, is the sublimest form) that is capable of precipitating this process by 'melting apparent surfaces away, and displaying the infinite which was hid' (*The Marriage*, pl. 14). The 'infinite that was hid' here corresponds to the eternal, the heaven in a wild flower. Art, prophecy and the forgiveness of sins are means by which individuals may escape from abstraction and the Polypus of materialism, and thereby re-enter the Body of Christ. Blake recognizes that each of these redemptive processes requires an imaginative response that can see beyond legislation: punishment and revenge can be legislated for – 'take life for life, eye for eye, tooth for tooth' (Exodus 21.23–5) – but love cannot be codified in a book; forgiveness cannot be legislated: 'Lord, how many times shall I forgive someone who sins against me? Up to seven times?' Peter asks Jesus. Jesus replies, 'I tell you, not seven times, but seventy-seven times' (Matthew 18.21–2).

Such matters require the imaginative act of compassion. It is because of the creative or imaginative quality of forgiveness, compassion and prophecy that Blake calls Jesus and his apostles 'artists'. Moreover, it is for this reason that Blake closely identifies 'art' with the forgiveness of sins: both are, in his view, creative and compassionate responses to human dilemmas. Art, for Blake, is the means whereby humanity may be seen in the eternal context of divine love: it is primarily to do with creative responses to human experience. It is therefore unsurprising that there are many widely admired 'artists' (such as Titian and Joshua Reynolds) whom Blake does not consider to be artists at all. Being technically skilled in an art is, for Blake, nothing in itself. Artistic technique only becomes meaningful when it is used to express a vision that is 'artistic' in the senses discussed above. For this reason, Blake, in his late work, the *Laocoön*, states that 'Prayer is the Study of Art. Praise is the Practise of Art' and 'Jesus & his Apostles & Disciples were all Artists'.

Error and perception

A key factor in this discussion is that error is a product of perception, a mistaken or limited perspective on eternity. Error therefore
remains invisible to us for as long as we assume that the way we see
is the way things are. As long as we think of the status quo as
'reality', we will never be able to change its pernicious aspects (this
is the situation of the *Innocence* chimney sweeper). To escape states
of error, then, Blake says, we first need to recognize them, and art is
a means to doing this because it is able to embody them. Once we
have embodied error by giving it a form, we can cast it out. Art is the
means to embodying the fallen aspects of ourselves and our society,
enabling us to act upon them by making them visible. One of Blake's
key targets is what he calls the 'single vision' of empiricism, and in
The Marriage he proposes a surprisingly pragmatic solution to this
form of perceptual error. He states the need for an enlargement of
the senses, an 'improvement of sensual enjoyment' (pl. 14, *E*38) that
will reveal the world of experience in its eternal aspect, for 'if the
doors of perception were cleansed every thing would appear to man
as it is: infinite' (pl. 14, *E*38). This cleansing process, Blake argues,
will be effected through the corrosive function of his own art, which
is capable of 'melting apparent surfaces away, and displaying the
infinite which was hid' (pl. 14, *E*38). This, of course, is also an allu-
sion to the processes of production of Blake's etched metal plate.

For Blake, art is something that should serve a redemptive
purpose, it is to be used and discarded, it is not part of eternity itself.
If we regard art as truth, we idolize it, and it enslaves us. Truth for
Blake is dynamic not static. The truth of art is that it can embody
error, thereby making error visible, and Blake represents this process
of embodiment and subsequent casting out in terms of a Last
Judgement. In the traditional biblical view, the Last Judgement is a
single universal apocalyptic event at the end of time when all people
are brought before God and judged according to their lives. In Blake,
however, the Last Judgement is an individual process that can be
effected at any moment; it is a moment of revelation when error is
exposed and truth revealed, and in that process, as in the forgiveness
of sins described above, we are restored (however temporarily) to the
divine, to eternity. In *Descriptions of the Last Judgment* Blake writes
that 'whenever any Individual Rejects Error & Embraces Truth[,] a
Last Judgment passes upon that Individual' (*E*562). This moment of

revelation, this exposure of eternity, is continuous with the heaven seen in a wild flower. Without this ongoing Last Judgement, Blake argues, error accumulates and eventually manifests in its most terrifying form as war. Hence in the *Laocoön* he writes: 'Art Degraded, Imagination Denied, War Governed the Nations'.

The universal family

Blake's politically and theologically charged alternative to the world of war and error is a society in which individuals – redeemed from the 'Satan' of a shallow, self-regarding materialism – co-exist as a 'universal family' that is united through the Imagination in the Divine Body:

> Mutual in one another's love and wrath all renewing
> We live as One Man; for contracting our infinite senses
> We behold multitude; or expanding: we behold as one,
> As One Man all the Universal Family; and that One Man
> We call Jesus the Christ: and he in us, and we in him,
> Live in perfect harmony in Eden the land of life,
> Giving, recieving, and forgiving each others trespasses. (*Jerusalem*,
> pl. 38, *E*179)

This is a dynamic vision, not one of stasis; it is about relationship and understanding such that opposition can be true friendship. As this passage shows, for Blake, to be in eternity, or to be redeemed, is to be in one's own humanity in relationship with the humanity of others. This vision of the indwelling of humanity in the divine has important biblical prefigurements, such as Jesus' prayer for those that shall believe in him, 'that all of them may be one, Father, just as you are in me and I am in you' (John 17.21).

The human perspective

From the empirical perspective, humanity appears to exist *within* the universe. However, Blake's vision of eternity contains no separate nature (*within* which humanity might exist). Nature, as discussed above, is neutral material for Blake, but it does function (as described earlier) as a mirror that can reflect to us our own humanity: the sun may appear as a guinea or as a host of angels. Blake resists the worship of an external nature as yet another scheme of abstraction, and he asserts that the spirits, wonders and beauties that are found in nature all ultimately come from the human heart. Historically, imaginative pagan engagements with nature have filled it with deities and spirits associated with woods, rivers, trees, and so on, but in time, Blake argues, people forgot the human origins of these imaginative visions, and thought they existed in and of themselves. This is the account Blake gives in *The Marriage* of how 'men forgot that All deities reside in the human breast.' (pl. 11, *E*37).

There is, for Blake, no means of describing nature apart from the human perspectives that we have on it (see pp. 64–7 above), and nature is therefore something interior to humans rather than exterior to them: its only perceivable life lies within us. The material universe therefore only takes shape as it is perceived: 'Nature has no Outline: but Imagination has. Nature has no Tune: but Imagination has! Nature has no Supernatural & dissolves: Imagination is Eternity' (*The Ghost of Abel*, *E*269). Thinking of nature as having a 'real' external existence outside of humanity is, for Blake, just another return to abstraction. Thus Blake writes:

all are Men in Eternity [. . .]
as in your own Bosom you bear your Heaven
And Earth, & all you behold, tho it appears Without it is Within
In your Imagination of which this World of Mortality is but a Shadow.
(*Jerusalem*, pl. 71, *E*224)

This presents one of the most conceptually challenging aspects of Blake's work, which is that when viewed from a 'cleansed' or 'eternal' perspective, all things will appear in relation to our humanity, because for them to take any other form would lead back into the cycle of abstraction discussed earlier. When we look at nature, what we see is our own humanity reflected, and each of us therefore sees slightly differently.

In a poem of 1800 enclosed in a letter to Thomas Butts, Blake describes a 'vision of light' that he had while sitting on the sands at Felpham:

To my Friend Butts I write
My first Vision of Light
On the yellow sands sitting

The Sun was Emitting
His Glorious beams
From Heavens high Streams
Over Sea over Land
My Eyes did Expand
Into regions of air
Away from all Care
Into regions of fire
Remote from Desire
The Light of the Morning
Heavens Mountains adorning
In particles bright
The jewels of Light
Distinct shone & clear –
Amazd & in fear
I each particle gazed
Astonishd Amazed
For each was a Man
Human formd. Swift I ran
For they beckond to me
Remote by the Sea
Saying. Each grain of Sand
Every Stone on the Land
Each rock & each hill
Each fountain & rill
Each herb & each tree
Mountain hill Earth & Sea
Cloud Meteor & Star
Are Men Seen [from] Afar (*E*711)

This poem seems strange at first, but Blake is showing what it might mean to go beyond the empirical view of nature, as he does when seeing a 'world in a grain of sand'. He is seeing nature in its eternal aspect here; he sees his own humanity, and that of others, reflected through it.

Blake's humanized vision inevitably laid him open to charges of madness that were made even during his own lifetime. Blake was quite aware of these accusations, and in *Descriptions of the Last Judgment* explained himself to an imagined interlocutor:

"What?" it will be Questiond, "When the Sun rises do you not see a round Disk of fire somewhat like a Guinea?" O no no, I see an Innumerable company of the Heavenly host crying Holy Holy Holy is the Lord God Almighty. I question not my Corporeal or Vegetative Eye any more than I would Question a Window concerning a Sight: I look thro it & not with it. (*E565–6*)

Here Blake recognizes that while we may see the same sun in terms of a common physiological response of light striking the retina, this is the beginning rather than the end of understanding. Newton is not in the sunlight.

PART FOUR: BLAKE'S FOURFOLD MYTH

The ideas of Blake's art discussed above are related to a central repeated narrative of his work. The basic myth of Blake's work is this: Albion, Blake's Everyman figure, has a being made up of four aspects: creativity, reason, passion and the heart. These are embodied as characters or 'Zoas' called, respectively, Urthona/Los, Urizen, Luvah and Tharmas. The fourfold division of the Zoas has many antecedents, including the four evangelists (Matthew, Mark, Luke and John), and the four beasts that surround God's throne in the visions of Ezekiel and of Revelation. In eternity, the four are in a constant productive relationship that Blake describes as 'spiritual warfare'. Periodically, however, one of them attempts to gain control of Albion. Blake's mythological works dramatize the process whereby one Zoa (one aspect of Albion) rises to dominance and causes chaos for a time before eventually being brought back into relationship with the others again. This is the narrative of *Urizen*.

   This is a simplified version of Blake's central myth (in actuality it is complicated by the fact that the Zoas can take different forms, turn into each other, and have spectres and emanations) but it is a helpful starting point to find a way into Blake. Moreover, the different prophetic books don't map neatly onto each other as Blake's mythology develops. For example, reason and energy are contrasted in *The Marriage*, and Jesus is associated there with creative energy. In *Urizen*, however, Urizen represents reason, and his contrary is Los, but Los doesn't then map back onto Jesus (except partially in *The Marriage*, as Blake-Los-artist identifies with the Jesus risen from the tomb).

The myth of Albion can be, and has been, read in many different ways, including psychobiographically (as a history of Blake's intellectual development), psychologically (as a depiction of mental growth and development), culturally (as a history of the rise of empiricism and the Enlightenment), and so on. The narratives concerning the Zoas are also multi-layered, and the interplay between the layers is not kept distinct. Thus Urizen can be read as Jehovah, as Blake himself (as author), as reason, as the pre-eminence of Enlightenment thought in Blake's age, and so on.

The relationship of the Zoas to the person of Albion is the same as that of the members of the Church to the Body of Christ. Social division is a mental breakdown that occurs when, as in Paul's image, the whole body wants to be an eye or a foot. There is no longer a mutual relationship between the different members, instead there is tyranny and single vision. In his work, Blake attempts to give reign to all the Zoas: to write as a fully human artist, using colour, music (he sang his *Songs*), different genres, humour, epic, myth, and so on. He does not write theological treatises because he tries to avoid abstracting what he's saying, but instead he maintains the contingency and particularity of his creative work. Consequently, my own description of Blake is by its very form a partial misrepresentation of his art. His fourfold vision cannot be embodied in a narrative such as this chapter which attempts to 'explain' Blake. I have presented a Urizenic rationalization of his work that can deliver only a partial perspective on what he offers.

STUDY QUESTIONS

1. Does Blake idealize the human? Read 'A Divine Image' and 'The Human Abstract' in *Songs of Experience*. How do these poems relate to the claims made about the human in this chapter?
2. Read 'A Poison Tree' in *Songs of Experience*. How does this relate to the discussion of forgiveness above?
3. Look at 'The Little Boy Lost' and 'The Little Boy Found' in *Songs of Innocence*. How do these relate to the discussion of abstract and human conceptions of God in this chapter?

CHAPTER 4

CRITICAL RECEPTION AND PUBLISHING HISTORY

PRINTING METHOD

The original copper plates on which Blake etched and engraved his illuminated books have not survived (with the exception of one corner of a discarded plate for *America*), and there is little contemporary written evidence giving specific details of his etching methods. Blake left some written explanations in his Notebook of how to perform different types of engraving task, but he did not leave an account of how he created his illuminated books. The issue has become more mysterious because an early biographical report stated that Blake had been taught his method of book production by his younger brother Robert:

> Blake, after deeply perplexing himself as to the mode of accomplishing the publication of his illustrated songs, without their being subject to the expense of letter-press, his brother Robert stood before him in one of his visionary imaginations, and so decidedly directed him in the way in which he ought to proceed, that he immediately followed his advice, by writing his poetry, and drawing his marginal subjects of embellishments in outline upon the copper-plate with an impervious liquid, and then eating the plain parts or lights away with aquafortis considerably below them, so that the outlines were left as stereotype. (John Thomas Smith, *Nollekens and his Times*, 1828, quoted in *Blake Records*, 609)

There may seem nothing strange in this, except that Robert had been dead for some years when he gave the explanation. There has been a good deal of experimentation by printmakers (including the Spanish artist Joan Miró) and scholars to work out Blake's methods, and the account which follows is entirely based on the very detailed work of Robert N. Essick in *William Blake: Printmaker*, and particularly on Joseph Viscomi's account in *Blake and the Idea of the Book*.

Blake bought copper in large sheets which were cut to size either by being scored and snapped, or 'by being cut with a hammer and chisel on an anvil' (*Viscomi*, 48). The plates were polished to a mirror surface using pumice, charcoal, and finally oil and felt, and the surface was then degreased using either stale bread, ammonia and whiting (ground chalk), or dilute nitric acid (*Viscomi*, 48–9). This allowed the ink to grip the sheet, and, if nitric acid was used, it would have created a matt key to the surface, making it easier to work on. In normal etching practice the whole plate would be coated with an even acid-resistant ground which, once dry, would take a design scratched into it using an engraving needle. In creating the illuminated books, however, Blake worked in a different manner. No ground was used, but instead the design and reverse-writing were applied with brush and pen, using stop-out varnish – probably either a natural bitumen such as asphalt, or ground resin dissolved in turpentine or alcohol. This may have been mixed with an oil to slow down the drying process so that the fluid would not harden on the brush (*Viscomi*, 53).

The writing was probably executed using a normal quill, and the illustrations drawn on with the same, then washed or detailed with brushes (*Viscomi*, 57ff). When the ink had dried it would be hard and could be scratched into with a needle, allowing fine detail to be added. The hardening quality of the stop-out varnish also meant that it could be chipped off and reapplied, giving some scope for the correction of errors. After the design had been completed, a wax wall was built around the edge of the plate, and acid (probably nitric) was poured in. The reaction of copper and acid produces gas bubbles, which were removed using a feather to ensure that there was no pitting of the plate. When the bite was sufficiently deep (only about a tenth of a millimetre) the plate was removed from the acid, rinsed thoroughly, and the stop (which would have remained on the plate) was removed with turpentine. The creation of the plate was now complete, and it was ready to be inked and used for printing (*Viscomi*, 78ff).

Unusually for an engraver, Blake owned his own press, which allowed him to experiment with inking and printing in a way which would not have been possible had he passed the work on to a professional printer. He used the same etched plates for two quite different methods of printing, to produce either monochrome or colour prints. When printing in colour, Blake used an unusual intaglio method, in which the plates were inked with colours made from pigment mixed with water and warm diluted size (a sort of glue). The colour was applied with short-hair brushes to the relief design of the plate, as well as to the etched shallows (*Viscomi*, 121). The design acted as a template demarcating different areas to be filled with colour, and the impression was then taken using the intaglio printing method in which the damp paper is forced by the press into the etched shallows of the plate (*Viscomi*, 99). This meant that the whole plate would print rather than just the outline of the design. Because of the pressure required by intaglio printing, the paper generally received a plate mark which was a sufficiently deep indentation to prevent it from being printed on the reverse side (*Viscomi*, 103). Perhaps because of this, Blake printed the majority of his illuminated books in monochrome and coloured them later by hand. These monochrome prints were produced by a relief printing method, in which the inking procedure was considerably simpler. Rather than using brushes to ink the plates, Blake employed a stiff linen dabber which would do the job quickly and evenly (*Viscomi*, 101). The monochrome print could then be taken using much less pressure on the press because the paper did not need to be forced into the design, but only to pick up the ink from its relief surface. This meant that the plate mark was no longer present, and it enabled Blake to print on both sides of the paper, permitting a more satisfactory format for his books (*Viscomi*, 105). Blake usually finished his prints by hand: monochrome prints were often detailed or coloured in ink and watercolour, and this became a necessity in the case of the colour prints because of the rather clumsy method of their execution. The thick inks and substantial pressure of the press often blurred the images, and they generally needed to be redefined using a pen (*Viscomi*, 121). Blake used a high-quality wove paper for his prints, which was sized so that it would take watercolour. The paper was dampened the day before printing in order to enable it to take the impression more easily (*Viscomi*, 99). Once the prints had dried, they were collated, pierced with three holes through the left-hand margin, and bound between two sheets of paper with string (*Viscomi*, 149).

HOW BLAKE SOLD THE BOOKS AND PRINTS

The majority of Blake's illuminated works were sold to private collectors, such as his patron Thomas Butts. He had hoped to be able to produce many copies easily, but the numbers of extant illuminated books is actually quite small. The traditional view of Blake is that he was unknown during his own lifetime, though this wasn't quite the case:

> [T]here is plentiful evidence of [Blake having a] contemporary audience. In 1794, Joseph Johnson, one of the foremost progressive publishers of the decade, was displaying Blake's books for prospective customers. Bentley's *Blake Books* lists sixty-one persons who bought copies of the illuminated books in Blake's lifetime or shortly after. Blair's *Grave* (1808) with Blake's illustrations had no fewer than 578 subscribers. (Davies and Schuchard, 36)

Nonetheless, these are tiny numbers compared to the sales of contemporaries such as Byron. Blake did make some attempt to sell his works to the public, and in 1793 he wrote his only public advertisement, a prospectus entitled 'To the Public' advertising the works he then had in print:

1. Job, a Historical Engraving. Size 1 ft.7½ in. by 1ft. 2 in.: price 12*s*.
2. Edward and Elinor, a Historical Engraving. Size 1 ft. 6½ in. by 1 ft.: price 10*s*. 6*d*.
3. America, a Prophecy, in Illuminated Printing. Folio, with 18 designs: price 10*s*. 6*d*.
4. Visions of the Daughters of Albion, in Illuminated Printing. Folio, with 8 designs, price 7*s*. 6*d*.
5. The Book of Thel, a Poem in Illuminated Printing. Quarto, with 6 designs, price 3*s*.
6. The Marriage of Heaven and Hell, in Illuminated Printing. Quarto, with 14 designs, price 7*s*. 6*d*.

7. Songs of Innocence, in Illuminated Printing. Octavo, with 25 designs, price 5*s*.
8. Songs of Experience, in Illuminated Printing. Octavo, with 25 designs, price 5*s*.
9. The History of England, a small book of Engravings. Price 3*s*.
10. The Gates of Paradise, a small book of Engravings. Price 3*s*. (*E*692)

Blake's production numbers remained small. Between 1789 and 1795, by far the most prolific period of illuminated book production in Blake's life (representing three quarters of all his known illuminated works), Blake produced only 125 copies of 15 different books (*Viscomi*, 372). The illuminated books remained a sideline to regular employment in commercial engraving, and never became his chief occupation for any sustained period. Given the length of time taken to produce these works, and the disproportionately low price that Blake asked for them, it would never have been financially viable for him to rely on them as his principal source of income (*Viscomi*, 154). In 1793, the year of publication of *The Marriage*, Blake was asking five shillings for a unique hand-coloured copy of *Songs of Innocence* printed in an 'edition' of perhaps 17 copies, which was the same price as the first edition of Wordsworth and Coleridge's *Lyrical Ballads* published five years later, without illustration, in an edition of 500 copies (*Viscomi*, 155).

'To the Public' also explains Blake's rationale in choosing to produce and print illuminated books. Blake writes:

The Labours of the Artist, the Poet, the Musician, have been proverbially attended by poverty and obscurity; this was never the fault of the Public, but was owing to a neglect of means to propagate such works as have wholly absorbed the Man of Genius. Even Milton and Shakespeare could not publish their own works. This difficulty has been obviated by the Author of the following productions now presented to the Public; who has invented a method of Printing both Letter-press and Engraving in a style more ornamental, uniform, and grand, than any before discovered, while it produces works at less than one fourth of the expense.

If a method of Printing which combines the Painter and the Poet is a phenomenon worthy of public attention, provided that it exceeds in elegance all former methods, the Author is sure of his reward. (*E*691)

The passage suggests that Blake believed the real challenge facing him as an artist to be one of production and distribution. Solve these matters, he thought, and he would be 'sure of his reward'. What he failed to take into account was that his social and professional status, class and psychological reputation might all be taken into consideration by potential buyers. The prejudices that he met with in these different areas *were* very much 'the fault of the public'. Chapter 1 suggested that the support given to Blake by the Mathew Circle may have been accompanied by a degree of condescension or even patronization, and the evidence suggests that Blake met with similar responses in his later life. As an artisan, an engraver, who had not been to university, Blake was simply not in the same social position as contemporary poets such as Byron, Shelley, Wordsworth or Coleridge, and his work was not considered in the same way. This issue is brought into focus by Blake's standing at the Royal Academy.

THE ROYAL ACADEMY

The Royal Academy was founded in 1768 by George III, with the aim of promoting the arts in Britain. It held (and still holds) annual exhibitions and, as discussed in Chapter 1, Blake had entered there as a student engraver, taking life classes and attending lectures. There was discrimination in the Academy between, on the one hand, 'artists' (such as painters and sculptors) who were considered to be 'inventors' and, on the other hand, 'craftsmen' (particularly engravers) whose work was to 'copy', to 'reproduce'. The distinction between the two types of artist was written into the Royal Academy's constitution, and engravers were unable to become fellows of the Royal Academy.

The Royal Academy's attitude influenced, and was continuous with, wider public opinions about what constituted a real artist. Because his work was not popular, and because he was an engraver (rather than a painter), Blake was unable to exhibit his work at major galleries or exhibitions, such as those of the Royal Academy. As a result, his only real option was to hang a private exhibition. He could not afford the expense of renting exhibition rooms, so he held his only private exhibition (1809–10) in his brother James's shop. He exhibited three rooms of pictures (about 16 pieces), and wrote an accompanying programme entitled *A Descriptive Catalogue* (*E*525ff). The catalogue is quite a strange item because it not only describes the pieces themselves, but it also makes strident claims about Blake's own genius and the merits and faults of major artists. Blake begins his preface:

THE eye that can prefer the Colouring of Titian and Rubens to that of Michael Angelo and Rafael, ought to be modest and to doubt its own powers. Connoisseurs talk as if Rafael and Michael Angelo had never seen the colouring of Titian or Correggio: They ought to know that Correggio was born two years before Michael Angelo, and Titian but four years after. Both Rafael and Michael Angelo knew the Venetian, and contemned and rejected all he did with the utmost disdain, as that which is fabricated for the purpose to destroy art.

Mr. B. appeals to the Public, from the judgment of those narrow blinking eyes, that have too long governed art in a dark corner. The eyes of stupid cunning never will be pleased with the work any more than with the look of self-devoting genius. (*E*528)

Blake's desire to attack iconic painters such as Titian in his catalogue makes more sense in the light of the artistic denigration of engravers discussed above, as does his defence of outline, the sharp definition and edges that characterize Blake's pictures. Outline was intrinsic to Blake's engraved work, and presented a strong technological difference from the more liquid, tonal qualities of oil paint. Blake writes of one of his own pieces:

The character and expression in this picture could never have been produced with Ruben's light and shadow, or with Rembrandt's, or any thing Venetian or Flemish. The Venetian and Flemish practice is broken lines, broken masses, and broken colours. Mr. B.'s practice is unbroken lines, unbroken masses, and unbroken colours. Their art is to lose form, his art is to find form, and to keep it. His arts are opposite to theirs in all things. (*E*537)

No matter how justified this sort of defence of engraving may have been, it was bound to elicit a negative reaction from those who already held strong views on art, and it did.

1790–1827: CRITICAL RESPONSES DURING BLAKE'S LIFETIME

Blake's catalogue was of great interest to some well-known figures of the day, particularly the essayist Charles Lamb and the diarist Henry Crabb Robinson. Both of these writers were fascinated by Blake and his exhibition, but unfortunately did not publish public reviews of it in English. The only press review that Blake's exhibition received at the time was that of the critic Robert Hunt, the brother of Leigh Hunt. In the periodical the *Examiner*, Hunt attacked Blake in forthright and unfeeling terms, writing:

> WILLIAM BLAKE, an unfortunate lunatic, whose personal inoffensiveness secures him from confinement, and, consequently, of whom no public notice would have been taken, if he was not forced on the notice and animadversion of the EXAMINER, in having been held up to public admiration by many esteemed amateurs and professors as a genius in some respect original and legitimate. The praises which these gentlemen bestowed last year on this unfortunate man's illustrations of *Blair's Grave*, have, in feeding his vanity, stimulated him to publish his madness more largely, and thus exposed him, if not to the derision, at least to the pity of the public. . . . Thus encouraged, the poor man fancies himself a great master, and has painted a few wretched pictures, some of which are unintelligible allegory, others an attempt at sober character by caricature representation, and the whole "blotted and blurred," and very badly drawn. These he calls an Exhibition, of which he has published a Catalogue, or rather a farrago of nonsense, unintelligibleness, and egregious vanity, the wild effusions of a distempered brain. (Quoted in *Bentley*, 333)

This review had a powerful effect on Blake, who never held another exhibition (though he did submit four pictures to the 1812 exhibition of the Associated Painters in Water Colour). Blake responded, in part, by incorporating the three Hunt brothers into his epic *Jerusalem*, and giving them the names of the accusers of Socrates

(*Bentley*, 313). He was clearly wounded by the attack, but he may also have anticipated it. Even within the catalogue itself he writes:

> The execution of my Designs, being all in Water-colours, (that is in Fresco) are regularly refused to be exhibited by the *Royal Academy*, and the *British Institution* has, this year, followed its example, and has effectually excluded me by this Resolution; I therefore invite those Noblemen and Gentlemen, who are its Subscribers, to inspect what they have excluded: and those who have been told that my Works are but an unscientific and irregular Eccentricity, a Madman's Scrawls, I demand of them to do me the justice to examine before they decide. (*E526–7*)

The first biography of Blake appeared in 1806 in Benjamin Heath Malkin's *A Father's Memoirs of His Child*. The account praises Blake, and yet at the same time the author writes:

> Mr. Blake has long been known to the order of men among whom he ranks; and is highly esteemed by those, who can distinguish excellence under the disguise of singularity. Enthusiastic and high flown notions on the subject of religion have hitherto, as they usually do, prevented his general reception, as a son of taste and of the muses. The sceptic and the rational believer, uniting their forces against the visionary, pursue and scare a warm and brilliant imagination, with the hue and cry of madness. Not contented with bringing down the reasonings of the mystical philosopher, as they well may, to this degraded level, they apply the test of cold calculation and mathematical proof to departments of the mind, which are privileged to appeal from so narrow and rigorous a tribunal. They criticise the representations of corporeal beauty, and the allegoric emblems of mental perfections; the image of the visible world, which appeals to the senses for a testimony to its truth, or the type of futurity and the immortal soul, which identifies itself with our hopes and with our hearts, as if they were syllogisms or theorems, demonstrable propositions or consecutive corollaries. By them have the higher powers of this artist been kept from public notice, and this genius tied down, as far as possible, to the mechanical department of his profession. (Quoted in *Blake Records*, 564–5)

Malkin, even at this midway stage of Blake's career, recognizes the unacceptability of the form of Blake's work to certain audiences (such as the Hunts), the lack of sympathy his work will be met with, the charge of 'madness' that it will engender, and the contemporary denigration of engraving: 'the mechanical department of his profession'. Malkin also picks up on Blake's biblical and prophetic aspirations. Following a discussion of 'Holy Thursday' from *Songs of Innocence*, he writes:

> The devotional pieces of the Hebrew bards are clothed in that simple language, to which Johnson with justice ascribes the character of sublimity. There is no reason therefore, why the poets of other nations should not be equally successful, if they think with the same purity, and express themselves in the same unaffected terms. (Quoted in *Blake Records*, 567–8)

Malkin here clearly grasps the aspiration of Blake's art (as poet-prophet) that Hunt entirely fails to understand.

Although Crabb Robinson did not publish an account of Blake's work in English following the exhibition, he did publish an article in German, in a German magazine entitled *Vaterländisches Museum*, in 1811. The piece discusses Blake's life, praises his work, notes his religious inspiration and non-conformist background, and tries to make sense of the 'Descriptive Catalogue'. It contests (though not directly) Hunt's charges, but this had little impact as the article was not published in English.

In the case of most major authors – writers such as Wordsworth or Byron – an account of contemporary critical responses might require distinguishing between public reactions to the author's work, and those of his or her fellow artists. In Blake's case this doesn't quite apply because he was scarcely known to the public during his lifetime, and most of the contemporary responses we have to Blake's art are, perhaps surprisingly, from well-known writers, printers, publishers or critics of the day. Many of these contacts were due to Crabb Robinson, who knew so many of the literary figures of Blake's era, had taken Lamb to Blake's exhibition, and later introduced his work to Hazlitt (*Bentley*, 133) and perhaps to Southey (*Bentley*, 339). Crabb Robinson only met Blake in 1825 (*Bentley*, 337), but had read his work much earlier. Coleridge may also have met Blake, though this is not certain. What is sure is that Coleridge had read *Songs of Innocence* by 1818, as on 6 February of that year he wrote in a letter:

> I have this morning been reading a strange publication – viz.
> Poems with very wild and interesting pictures, as the swathing,
> etched (I suppose) but it is said – printed and painted by the
> Author, W. Blake. He is a man of Genius – and I apprehend, a
> Swedenborgian – certainly, a mystic *emphatically*. (*Bentley*, 351)

Wordsworth also read at least some of Blake's poems from *Innocence* and *Poetical Sketches* (*Bentley*, 133). Malkin's short biography (discussed above) contained examples of Blake's verse, and it is from this volume that Wordsworth and his sister Dorothy copied some of Blake's poems into a commonplace book in 1807 (*Blake Records*, 571*n*). Something of Wordsworth's response to Blake is also recorded by Crabb Robinson, who reported:

> I read W[ordsworth] some of Blake's poems[;] he was pleased
> with Some of them and consid[ere]d B[lake] as hav[in]g the ele-
> ments of poetry – a thousand times more than either Byron or
> Scott. (Quoted in *Bentley*, 342)

Crabb Robinson is also the source of one of the other scarce responses we have of Wordsworth to Blake. He reports Wordsworth as saying of the latter:

> There is no doubt this poor man was mad, but there is something
> in the madness of this man which interests me more than the
> Sanity of Lord Byron & Walter Scott. (Quoted in *Bentley*, 380)

Apart from the interest Blake received later in life from 'the Ancients' (the small group of devotees mentioned in Chapter 1), the restriction of his audience to a limited number of fellow artists and collectors remained true even for some time after his death in 1827. What is perhaps most surprising is that the next generation of collectors to become interested in Blake were also creators in their own right, and they included some of the most important figures in Victorian art and literature: the Rossetti family.

1827–1900: CRITICAL RECEPTION AND PUBLISHING HISTORY

In 1828, the year after Blake's death, John Thomas Smith (who had known Blake personally for many years) wrote an appreciative short biography in a book entitled *Nollekens and his Times*. Smith's account discusses the accusations of madness, Robert's inspiration of Blake's methods, Blake's everyday life and habits, some particular works, and the poet's death and funeral. It was written when Catherine – whom Smith also discusses – was still alive. Two years later, in another biography, Allan Cunningham extended the material recounted by Smith, and also attempted to discuss *Urizen* and *Jerusalem*, but appears to have been confused by them. The real importance of Cunningham's biography, however, is that it was printed in a very popular book (both in Britain and America) entitled *Lives of the Most Eminent British Painters, Sculptors, and Architects* (1830). It was through reading this widely circulated book that Dante Gabriel Rossetti, the Pre-Raphaelite poet and painter, became interested in Blake (*Dorfman*, 59). Rossetti's interest was such that in 1847 he bought Blake's Notebook from William Palmer – Samuel Palmer's brother – who at that time worked in the British Museum (*Dorfman*, 59–60). This purchase of Blake's Notebook (sometimes called 'The Rossetti Manuscript') was enormously important. The Notebook contains poetry, drawings, epigrams, and so on, and these include pieces in which Blake extends the attack on famous artists that had featured in his exhibition catalogue. He also takes the time to attack Sir Joshua Reynolds, and the institute of which he was president, the Royal Academy itself:

To English Connoisseurs

You must agree that Rubens was a Fool
And yet you make him master of Your School
And give more money for his Slobberings
Than you will give for Rafaels finest Things (*E*512)

William Rossetti said that the Notebook gave courage to the nascent Pre-Raphaelite Brotherhood in dismissing centuries of art, and thereby developing their own aesthetic (*Dorfman*, 60).

Given the limited knowledge about Blake's illuminated books and poetry at this time, the history of his manuscripts (such as the Rossetti Manuscript) is particularly important to his later reception. Some of these manuscripts fell into better hands than others. Frederick Tatham, one of the Ancients, inherited Blake's remaining papers and works from Catherine Blake at her death, but unfortunately – due to his religious convictions – he subsequently burned those that he thought were offensive (*Dorfman*, 52–3). Fortunately his destruction was not wholesale, and he later sold the surviving drawings to William Rossetti (*Dorfman*, 57). Through the Ancients, John Ruskin also came to know Blake's work, as he had become friends with one of their group, George Richmond (*Dorfman*, 38).

Individual poems by Blake were printed in a number of places from 1806 to 1849, including a version of the *Songs* edited by James John Garth Wilkinson (London, 1839), and his work was discussed in a range of journals and magazines throughout the nineteenth century (*Dorfman*, 43). Following the short biographical accounts of Blake discussed above, the first full biography was written by Alexander Gilchrist and published in 1863 (*Dorfman*, 56). Gilchrist prepared extensively in writing this biography, and he interviewed those who had known Blake personally, such as the Ancients. It was published in two volumes, the first containing the biography, and the second containing an anthology of Blake's poetry edited by Dante Gabriel Rossetti, and 'an annotated catalogue of Blake's visual works compiled by [William] Michael Rossetti' (Holmes, xxii). Gilchrist's work became the standard Blake biography for a long time.

Prior to this publication, the Rossettis hadn't done much to ensure wider circulation of Blake's poetry, although Dante Gabriel had introduced the poet Algernon Swinburne to Blake's works in 1857 (*Dorfman*, 63). This introduction was important because Swinburne would write the first full critical appraisal of Blake's work – *William Blake: A Critical Essay* – in 1868. Swinburne presented quite a different perspective on Blake from Gilchrist (*Dorfman*, 90), who, under Palmer's influence (*Dorfman*, 71), had portrayed a Blake who would be acceptable to a contemporary Christian audience. Swinburne, however, was reading Blake as an Eastern Mystic, and comparing him to the American poet Walt Whitman (1819–92). In Deborah Dorfman's words:

By providing a ready analogy with a more available poet, Swinburne confirmed his portrait of the prophet of sensual liberty and of the Pantheist akin to Oriental mystical writers. (*Dorfman*, 160–1)

The similarity between Blake and Whitman seems to have been noticed by others too: Gilchrist had died (though only 33 years old) while in the final stages of writing the biography, and the work was completed by his wife, Anne Gilchrist. She would subsequently move to America to write a biography of Whitman with whom she became close friends (Holmes, xxxv).

William Michael Rossetti published an edition of the poetry entitled *The Poetical Works of William Blake with a Prefatory Memoir* in 1874, which became the standard edition for the next two decades. However, the most influential edition of Blake's writings in the nineteenth century may have been that of another pre-eminent poet of the period, William Butler Yeats. Yeats produced his edition in collaboration with Edwin J. Ellis who, like Blake, was a poet and painter. The Ellis-Yeats edition of 1893 (*Dorfman*, 192) was an influential, though unreliable, edition published in three volumes, including a biography and an account of 'The Symbolic System'. The historical importance of the edition is that it went beyond earlier critical appraisals of Blake by attempting to systematically elucidate the poet's mythology. What Yeats wanted out of Blake, and how he viewed Blake in an occult or mystical light, will be discussed in more detail in Chapter 5.

1900–60: CRITICAL RECEPTION AND PUBLISHING HISTORY

A more reliable edition of Blake was produced by John Simpson in his *Poetical Works* of 1905 (*Dorfman*, 107), though this would be superseded when Geoffrey Keynes (brother of the economist John Maynard Keynes) edited a complete Blake in 1925, which was the basis of the widely used Keynes edition which is still in print today. However, the major development of the twentieth century was not so much the appearance of more reliable texts, as the advent of what have come to be the biggest propagators of the Blake industry: university English departments. English was at this time still a comparatively new academic subject, having only become established in

Oxford in 1894 and Cambridge in 1911. Ellis and Yeats had set the scene for the exposition of Blake's system, and the university offered an environment in which individuals could make a whole career of the systematic exposition of a particular author's work. At this time much of the focus of interest on Blake shifted from Britain to North America, and this was the context of one of the first, and best-known attempts to expound systematically Blake's ideas, and to relate him to his context: S. Foster Damon's *William Blake: His Philosophy and Symbols* of 1924.

A little over a decade later, the Canadian critic Northrop Frye began to compile the study of Blake that would be published in 1947 as *Fearful Symmetry: A Study of William Blake*. This is one of the most influential critical works ever to have been written on Blake and, although it is quite a difficult work, it gained the reputation (along with works by Damon and David Erdman) as one of the three key critical texts on Blake. The difficulty of *Fearful Symmetry* is that Frye is using Blake to try to work out a larger theory of literature which would be more fully developed in Frye's later work, and which moves towards an archetypal mode of criticism called 'myth criticism'. This sense-making, pattern-making approach to Blake's mythology has been a common feature of the criticism of his work, and it has developed alongside a different, but equally vigorous, tradition of interpretation, which has sought to schematize the meaning of Blake's books by relating them to their social and political contexts. Early works in this tradition include Mark Schorer's *William Blake: The Politics of Vision* of 1946, and Jacob Bronowski's *A Man without a Mask* of 1944. However, the book that really epitomizes the approach is David Erdman's *Blake: Prophet against Empire* of 1954. Erdman sets Blake's works within very specific social and political contexts, and tends to read the mythological elements as allegories of contemporary political or social situations. Erdman is also important for having edited a major edition of Blake's writings, *The Complete Poetry and Prose of William Blake* (1965) which has now taken the place of Keynes as the standard edition.

1960–2006: CRITICAL RECEPTION AND PUBLISHING HISTORY

In the latter part of the twentieth century there continued to be a strong critical interest in relating Blake to intellectual traditions or

world-views such as Freudian psychoanalysis, Jungian psychother-
apy, Marxism, alchemy, and so on, showing how his work anticipates, echoes or draws on these traditions. However, Blake studies
grew to be more strongly dominated by works in the tradition of
Erdman that have sought to relate Blake's books to their specific
socio-political contexts. This tradition is characterized by the
ongoing critical quest (defining itself against other modes of Blake
criticism) of putting Blake back into a proper historical context. To
take examples from three decades: in the 1970s Robert N. Essick and
Donald Pearce edited a collection of essays entitled *Blake in his Time*
(1978); in the 1980s there was a major exhibition (New Haven and
Toronto) entitled *William Blake: His Art and Times*; in the 1990s,
Steve Clark and David Worrall published two anthologies of essays,
Historicizing Blake (1994) and *Blake in the Nineties* (1999); and this
type of work continues to be a major element of Blake criticism in
the twenty-first century. One of the characteristics of this tradition
is suggested by Bindman's introduction to the book which accompanied the exhibition mentioned above. He writes:

> The notion that Blake was a naïf either as a poet or a painter – a
> 'semi-taught Dreamer', 'delivering the burning messages of
> prophecy by the stammering lips of infancy' – has long since been
> abandoned. Thanks to modern scholarship the sophisticated
> nature of his genius and his profound debt to writers and artists
> of the past are now obvious. (Bindman, 10)

Bindman's phrase 'modern scholarship' is about a professional, spe-
cialized approach to Blake that takes the artist out of the hands of
new-agers, enthusiasts, amateurs and the public at large (more of
whom in Chapter 5), and keeps him safely with the academics. This
separation of 'professional' responses to Blake has been emphasized
further by the development of new critical theories and methodolo-
gies in academic circles. This, combined with the changing values
and interests within literary studies, has meant that the schematiza-
tions of Blake by major critics of earlier in the twentieth century are
also now being brought into question. As Mike Goode puts it:

> Over the last two decades, critical consensus gradually has shifted
> to favor the idea of Blake's a- or even anti-systematicity, effec-

tively dismantling the unified systems that influential mid-century studies by Northrop Frye, S. Foster Damon, A. L. Morton, David Erdman, Harold Bloom, Kathleen Raine, Christine Gallant, and W. J. T. Mitchell proposed were organizing the illuminated books. (Goode, 772)

Many of the critical works on Blake published over the last twenty years are so difficult to read, and require such a specialist background to understand, that it sometimes seems that 'public' and 'professional' versions of Blake may have split apart irrevocably, and this in turn raises questions over the democratic commitments of criticism itself. Nonetheless, there have also been points at which the 'public' and 'professional' have been very successfully brought together. Most notable, perhaps, was the Blake exhibition held at the Tate Britain in 2000–1. It was the largest ever exhibition of Blake's work and attracted huge interest, and this extended interest has been served by the Internet, which has given new levels of accessibility to his work. David Erdman generously made Blake's *Complete Poetry and Prose* available online, and three major Blake scholars – Morris Eaves, Robert Essick and Joseph Viscomi – have overseen the Blake Archive, a superb online resource giving high-quality facsimiles of not just all the different illuminated books, but also different versions of the different illuminated books. Blake has never been more widely available to the public than he is today. The 'public' response to Blake is the subject of Chapter 5.

STUDY QUESTION

What is the price of Experience do men buy it for a song
Or wisdom for a dance in the street? No it is bought with the price
Of all that a man hath his house his wife his children
Wisdom is sold in the desolate market where none come to buy
And in the witherd field where the farmer plows for bread in vain (*E*324)

1. Read the quotation above. How does an understanding of Blake's printing methods and the struggle and criticism that he encountered in selling his books help in understanding the tone and themes of his works?

CHAPTER 5

ADAPTATION, INTERPRETATION AND INFLUENCE

Chapter 4 outlined the tradition of scholarly, editorial and critical responses to Blake's works. Although this has been dominated by the university, and although Blake is such a major figure within the canon of English literature, his influence extends far beyond such educational contexts and he has a substantial and ongoing cultural impact in many other fields. A number of the critics that I discussed earlier – such as the Rossettis, Swinburne and Yeats – were of course poets themselves, and their creative responses to Blake are continuous with a very different, and often more radical, tradition of appropriation and interpretation of his work among artists, pop stars, film-makers and novelists. This chapter provides an overview of these other types of engagement with Blake. Whereas Blake's contemporaries, such as Byron and Wordsworth, had an enormous and diverse impact on nineteenth-century culture, in Blake's case his cultural presence only really began to proliferate in the 1950s. Because the history of this impact is relatively short (really only the last 50 years) but very widespread, I have organized this chapter thematically rather than chronologically.

POETRY AND VISUAL ARTS

Poetic and visual imagery are inseparable in Blake's major works, his illuminated books. Few artists work easily in both media – Dante Gabriel Rossetti was one – fewer still combine them in the way that Blake does. One of the difficulties of assessing Blake's impact in the visual arts is that he worked in such a unique set of media: hand-coloured, engraved or etched illuminated books. As a result, there was never likely to be a school of Blake producing illuminated prophecies in the way that there have been schools of, say, cubism or impressionism. One of the aims of Blake's art that shaped its form was that he was attempting to devise an etching and printing process that could produce large numbers of illuminated books. Such methods are now redundant due to technological advances in mass colour reproduction of text and images. As a result, it is difficult to say what the closest present-day analogue to Blake's books would be, but one contender must be the comic strip. Like Blake's books, the comic strip combines text and illustration, tends to be focused on images of the human form, and often deals with themes that might be called, in the very broadest sense, 'apocalyptic'. One of the best-known authors working in this genre is the graphic novelist Alan Moore, who has cited Blake as an influence and released a perfor-mance CD entitled 'Angel Passage' organized around a narrative of Blake's visionary life.[1] Although Moore is a writer rather than an illustrator, the format of his work is visual (as in the graphic novel and now film version of *V for Vendetta*).

In terms of the imagery itself, the most explicit of Blake's follow-ers was Samuel Palmer, and Palmer's earlier work has something of the visionary intensity of Blake, but with a gentler pastoral tone. The similarity is most evident in relation to Blake's late woodcuts for an edition of *The Pastorals of Virgil* (*c.* 1820), although these works are uncharacteristically reticent for Blake. Palmer would subsequently become a substantial influence on British artists such as Paul Nash (1889–1946) and Eric Ravilious (1903–42), and one might argue that there is a lineage here from Blake through Palmer into these later British artists (Dent and Whittaker, 39–40). The link is precarious, however, as the tone of, say, one of Ravilious's small, gentle wood engravings could not be further from the apocalyptic violence of the images of a work such as *Urizen*.

One recent reinterpretation of Blake's visual work that comes much closer to the striking tone of its original is Eduardo Paolozzi's *Newton* (1995), which stands in the courtyard of the British Library. It is a huge bronze statue, closely based on Blake's 1795 image of the famous scientist whom Blake depicts as a Urizenic figure dividing up the universe. In a context that might be expected to celebrate learn-ing (the British Library), this massive statue appears to satirize the 'single vision' of science: Paolozzi has created an icon of ambivalence in a very different medium to Blake's own, but one which remains in close dialogue with it.

The impact of Blake's writing on later poetry is as difficult to be specific about as the influence of his art. No one else has ever written anything quite like *Jerusalem* or *Milton* and they provide neither an easy nor an obvious style to emulate. Of the artists discussed so far in this book, Yeats is closer than most to Blake in his attempt to develop an all-engulfing mystical or mythological system, particularly in later works such as *A Vision* (1925). It is perhaps no coincidence that this is also one of the few works that can rival *Jerusalem* in its obscurity and its challenge to readers. Nonetheless, this sort of poetic or mystical response to Blake maintained a strong presence later in the twentieth century, particularly in the work of the Beat poet Allen Ginsberg, whose poem *Howl* (1956) is markedly influenced by Blake. Work by Ginsberg and other US artists would subsequently impact on the British scene, bringing Blake's influence full-circle back to poets of his own country. Dent and Whittaker write:

> The liberatory counter-culture of 1960s America espoused by Ginsberg was transmitted across the Atlantic via his participation in the first International Poetry Incarnation at the Albert Hall in June 1965 [. . .] That event crystallized the constellation of a 'secret' generation of British poets such as John Cotton, Dave Cunliffe and Michael Horowitz, proponents of jazz and oral poetry that had lain hidden during the critical atmosphere of the 1950s. Michael Horowitz (1935–) edited examples of this poetry in his 1969 collection *Children of Albion: Poetry of the 'Underground' in Britain* [. . .] to which was appended a series of 'Blakean' Afterwords. (Dent and Whittaker, 110)

MYSTICISM AND THE OCCULT

Even during his own lifetime, Blake attracted individuals who were interested in the occult. This was not because Blake himself was interested in occult practices (he wasn't), but because his ability to see 'visions' attracted – and still attracts – those who were interested in the supernatural and the spirit worlds. John Varley is the most notable example of one of Blake's friends who was a willing believer in the poet's visions, and Varley himself was a keen astrologer and wrote a book entitled *Zodiacal Physiognomy* in 1828, as well as col-laborating with Blake on a work entitled *Visionary Heads*, in which Blake sketched (from 'vision') portraits of famous historical figures.

Later in the Victorian period, some critics sought to interpret Blake's poetry as a form of 'automatic writing', and this was contin-uous with the wider Victorian interest in the occult described here by Dorfman:

> Thomson saw Blake's inspiration as Divine; but automatic writing had more profane than sacred adherents. (The time was one in which spiritist phenomena, even of the table-knocking sort, interested and were found convincing by the cultivated. Wilkinson, Patmore [briefly], W. B. Scott, Tennyson [briefly], his brother Frederick, Mrs. Browning, and others were firmly per-suaded; William Rossetti, Swinburne, D. G. Rossetti, Dickens, and Milnes attended seances in the 1860s.[)] (*Dorfman*, 182)

The Victorian interest in the occult took new organizational forms towards the end of the nineteenth century and became combined with syncretistic attempts to distil or combine diverse elements of different religious traditions. Yeats himself was a member of a syncretistic/occult society called The Order of the Golden Dawn, which he had joined in 1890, around the same time that he was pre-paring his edition of Blake. Yeats is quite explicit about his own per-spective on these matters:

> I believe in the practice and philosophy of what we have agreed to call magic, in what I must call the evocation of spirits, though I do not know what they are, in the power of creating magical illu-sions, in the visions of truth in the depths of the mind when the eyes are closed. (*W. B. Yeats: Selected Criticism*, 90)

Yeats is not interested in Blake only as a poet, but also as a mystic or visionary. Another key figure in the Golden Dawn (and enemy of Yeats) was Aleister Crowley, practitioner of 'sex magick', Satanist, and reputedly the 'wickedest man in the world', who often quotes from Blake in his work (Dent and Whittaker, 156–8). However, such traditions did not appeal to everyone. Another pre-eminent poet of the period, T. S. Eliot, can be seen distancing himself (through satire and criticism) from such influences in the section of *The Waste Land* dealing with 'Madame Sosostris, famous clairvoyante' and that of *Four Quartets* which disavows attempts 'To communicate with Mars, [and] converse with spirits' (Dry Salvages, 5). This dislike of the occult may account, in part, for Eliot's response to Blake registered in an essay which contains a patronizing dismissal of what Eliot conceives to be an eclecticism that would now be termed 'New Age':

> We have the same respect for Blake's philosophy [. . .] that we have for an ingenious piece of home-made furniture: we admire the man who has put it together out of the odds and ends about the house. (Eliot, *Selected Prose*, 171)

In other words, very little respect at all.

The interest in Blake as an occult or mystical writer was continued into the later twentieth century by a number of critics, including Kathleen Raine, who sought – particularly in *Blake and Tradition* (1968) – to align Blake with a wide range of alchemical and Neoplatonic traditions. Raine's work draws on that of Carl Jung (1875–1961), who had developed an understanding of the psyche and processes of psychological growth based on, among other things, a theory of archetypes – that is, a collective symbolism shared across time and across cultures through a 'collective unconscious'. Jung thought that all people have access to this symbolic resource that lies deep within them. Many readers have been struck by similarities between Blake's mythology and ideas of individual emancipation, and Jung's ideas about archetypes and individuation. This has led to quite a number of comparative studies of the two writers, as well as a number of 'Jungian' readings of Blake's works (see Chapter 6). This type of archetypal criticism is methodologically similar to Frye's *Fearful Symmetry*, although Frye disingenuously claims that he purposefully avoided reading Jung while preparing his text. Nonetheless, the fine line between his own approach and occult or Jungian readings of Blake is suggested by Frye's own work:

> According to Bacon the experimenter searches nature for its underlying principles or forms, and Bacon believed it probable that there were comparatively few of these forms, which, when discovered, would be to knowledge what an alphabet is to a

language. And, reading imagination for experiment and art for nature, Blake also seems to be striving for an 'alphabet of forms', a Tarot pack of pictorial visions which box the entire compass of the imagination in an orderly sequence. (Frye, 417)

The links between these mystical/occult/Jungian readings of Blake have not been restricted to scholars; there has been widespread appropriation of Blake in these terms in a popular context. To take Frye's own mention of tarot as an example: tarot cards were originally designed for games, and began to be used for the purposes of fortune-telling in the nineteenth century. The first tarot pack designed in England was the famous Rider-Waite deck (1909). A. E. Waite, the designer of the deck, was, like Yeats and Crowley, a key member of The Order of the Golden Dawn. That deck inspired many others, including a comparatively recent 'William Blake Tarot Deck' which uses a different image from Blake's works to illustrate each card. The designer of the deck reads Blake in a similar way to critics such as Raine, and explains that he believes that Blake's works represent, 'a profound metaphysical tool for personal and spiritual development'. He goes on:

In his many works of poetry and painting, Blake gradually defined a complex personal mythology in which godlike characters he called Zoas symbolize the divine aspects of the human psyche or soul. In the William Blake Tarot these archetypal figures and their mythic roles are depicted in what I call the Tarot Triumphs, which exactly correspond to the traditional Major Arcana, although many are renamed to reflect Blake's view of the Tarot concepts.[2]

Here Blake's work is shown (supposedly) to anticipate the modern tarot deck in a way that meshes quite comfortably with the work of Raine, Jung or Frye. Blake has often been treated as a proto-Freud or a proto-Marx in a similar way.

Despite this history of appropriation, Blake's own work is not centrally engaged with occult traditions, but rather, as I have argued, with the Bible. Yet despite, or perhaps because of, there being such a widespread interest in Blake from psychological and occult perspectives, his work has not carried across into theology.

Despite Blake's imaginativeness, hermeneutical insight, and degree of engagement as a biblical interpreter, he has been virtually ignored by theologians, even though one dictionary of biblical interpretation describes him as 'probably *the* most original interpreter of the Bible' (Coggins and Houlden, 92, my italics). Those books that do exist on Blake's theology have come principally from literary critics.

PSYCHOACTIVE DRUGS

Aleister Crowley's experiments in occultism, sex and mysticism also incorporated the use of drugs, and psychoactive substances came to feature strongly in the later twentieth-century reception of Blake. Again, this is not because of any interest in drugs on Blake's own part – unlike his contemporaries Coleridge and Thomas De Quincey, Blake didn't take what would now be termed 'recreational drugs', but a number of his disciples have. Most famously, the author of *Brave New World*, Aldous Huxley (1894–1963), was seriously interested in both Blake and mysticism, and was also a pioneer experimenter with hallucinogenic drugs, particularly mescaline and later LSD. His short book *The Doors of Perception* (1954) discusses Blake at a number of points, and takes its title from plate 14 of *The Marriage*, and his later work *Heaven and Hell* (1956) takes its title from the same work. Huxley thought that psychoactive drugs provided the means to cleansing 'the doors of perception', thereby establishing a mystical relationship between the individual and eternity.

Huxley's interest in drugs and in Blake were later shared by Allen Ginsberg, and in the fifties and sixties, the relationship between the experience of psychoactive drugs and the depiction of Blake's visions seemed to many readers an obvious and natural one. In 1977, Orbis Publishing Ltd of London produced a large glossy hardback entitled *William Blake: The Seer and His Visions*. It is a reproduction of over 138 of Blake's pictures, with a sustained and serious commentary on them. Nonetheless, the author, Milton Klonsky, finds it appropriate to begin his introduction with three pages discussing his first LSD trip, and how this helped him to understand Blake (Klonsky, 7–9).

MUSIC

Blake has had a substantial impact on one of the dominant art forms of the twentieth century: pop music. This may be because he has traditionally been understood as a rebel or radical who, particularly in the 'Proverbs of Hell', appears to preach a gospel of excess: 'The road of excess leads to the palace of wisdom' (pl. 7, *E*34), 'He who desires but acts not, breeds pestilence' (pl. 7, *E*34), 'Sooner murder an infant in its cradle than nurse unacted desires' (pl. 10, *E*37), and so on. His influence here, as elsewhere, has been diverse. Blake's poems have been set to folk music by artists including Ginsberg, who released an album of Blake's *Songs* in 1970 entitled *William Blake's Songs of Innocence and of Experience*. More recently, the US folk singer Greg Brown recorded an album entitled *Songs of Innocence and of Experience* (1992), and in a slightly different folk idiom, that of 'Celtic folk', Van Morrison's 'Let The Slave' uses lines from *The Four Zoas* on his 1998 album *A Sense of Wonder*.

The translation of the *Songs* to a folk idiom is a fairly obvious one. A more acoustically challenging interpretation of Blake is the translation of the text of *The Marriage* into a black metal/experimental context by the Norwegian band Ulver on their album *Themes from William Blake's The Marriage of Heaven & Hell* (1999). The metal/concept mix is extended by Bruce Dickinson (lead singer of Iron Maiden) on his 1998 solo album *The Chemical Wedding*, which contains a mixture of Blakean themes, and songs about Urizen and Jerusalem. Further experimental work can be found on the German electronic group Tangerine Dream's 1987 album *Tyger*. Punk, or at least post-punk musicians have also worked with Blake: Jah Wobble's 2000 ambient/reggae/folk mix *The Inspiration of William Blake* explores Wobble's debt to the poet, while the US singer Patti Smith has discussed Blake's influence on her work a number of times. Both musicians performed in the celebratory events that formed part of the 2000–1 Tate Blake exhibition.[3]

Not all such works use the text itself. *Songs of Innocence* (1968) and *Songs of Experience* (1969) are instrumental albums by the composer, arranger and producer David Axelrod. Other bands have taken chunks of Blake's texts as the basis for new songs: 'History', a song on The Verve's album *A Northern Soul* (1995), is a rewrite of Blake's 'London', while The Doors use Blake's 'Auguries of

Innocence' as the basis of their song 'End of the Night' (1967). The Doors had also taken their name from Blake, whom they had discovered via Huxley's *The Doors of Perception*. Pop has not been the only musical form to draw on Blake. The best-known musical setting of a Blake work is 'Jerusalem' (the lyric, not to be confused with the prophetic book of the same name), which was set to music by Hubert Parry in 1916, and by Edward Elgar in 1922. The British composer Benjamin Britten created a setting of 'The Sick Rose' from *Songs of Experience* in his *Serenade for Tenor, Horn and Strings* in 1943, and used more Blake, including texts from the *Songs*, 'Auguries of Innocence' and *The Marriage*, in *Songs and Proverbs of William Blake* in 1965. Another British composer, Ralph Vaughan-Williams, created settings for selections for *10 Blake Songs* in 1957. However, the most extensive musical treatment of the *Songs* is perhaps William Bolcom's *Songs of Innocence and of Experience* written over a period of 25 years (1956–81) and drawing on an eclectic range of musical genres in order to illuminate and explore Blake's work.

NOVELS

Blake turns up as an artist that protagonists are preoccupied with in several novels. The central figure of Joyce Cary's 1944 *The Horse's Mouth* quotes Blake throughout that work, and in Thomas Harris's 1981 thriller *Red Dragon*, the killer's obsession with Blake's painting *The Great Red Dragon and the Woman Clothed in the Sun*, leads to his breaking into the Brooklyn Museum and eating the work. Blake has turned up both as a character and as an influence in a number of works of fantasy fiction and science fiction. Philip José Farmer's sci-fi/fantasy series *World of Tiers* draws on Blake's mythology for the names of its characters (Urizen, Lord Urthona, Red Orc, and so on), and Blake was an important influence on one of the biggest literary successes of the 1990s, Philip Pullman's trilogy, *His Dark Materials*. Thematically, the most Blakean part of Pullman's trilogy is the third novel, *The Amber Spyglass* (2000), which also incorporates quotations from Blake as chapter epigraphs. In another British children's book, David Almond's *Skellig* (1998), two children encounter Blake's poetry in a faintly Blakean story about befriending a ruined angel. Other works, such as Neil Penswick's Dr Who novel, *The Pit*, take a step further by incorporating Blake himself as a character in the narrative. In Penswick's novel Blake plays a central role when, after falling into hell through a hole in Cambridge, he meets Dr Who and the pair have to escape a series of horrors, including blue-skinned women riding pterodactyls and a black magic ceremony in Jack the Ripper's London, before attempting to prevent Armageddon. A tricky situation, even for Blake.

Blake's influence is not, however, restricted to an Anglo-American context. Besides being translated into many languages, his work is taken up in the title of the 2003 novel, *Rouse Up O Young Men of the New Age!* by the Nobel prize-winner Kenzaburo Oe, a partially autobiographical work in which the Japanese author reflects on his relationship with his son (who has severe learning difficulties) in the light of Blake's poetry.

TELEVISION, THEATRE, FILM

Since the 1960s there have been numerous TV documentaries about Blake, some of which have attempted to represent his character on screen. Perhaps the most sustained and successful of these attempts has been Jack Shepherd's play *In Lambeth*, which dramatizes an imaginary encounter between Blake, Catherine, and Thomas Paine. Shepherd's play thoughtfully communicates much about Blake's life and ideas, and was made into an excellent television adaptation in 1995, starring Mark Rylance, Lesley Clare O'Neill and Bob Peck. This careful biographical treatment is unusual, however, and Blake is more commonly encountered on television and film in the form of visual quotation. An example occurs in an episode ('The Eligible Bachelor') of the renowned television series in which Jeremy Brett played Sherlock Holmes. In a key scene set in a theatre, part of the staging – a huge painting based on Blake's 'Elohim creating Adam' – falls and kills one of the characters. The image is chosen, presumably, not only because it's a suitably terrifying Blakean icon, but also because as an image of 'God' it functions humorously as a true deus ex machina.

The same sort of quotation of Blakean images occurs in film. Sam Raimi's 1981 *The Evil Dead* is a cult horror film in which five students become possessed by spirits and subsequently horribly murder each other. The possession is caused by them reading a 'Book of the Dead' which they have stumbled on in the cellar of an old shack in the woods. Amongst the diabolic-looking scrawls inside the book is a sketch of Blake's *The Great Red Dragon and the Woman Clothed in the Sun*. The same picture – an image of the beast from the Book of Revelation – is also at the centre of the novel *Red Dragon* mentioned above, which, in turn, has been made into two films, *Manhunter* (1986) and *Red Dragon* (2002).

Blake's poetry seems to be just as quotable as his images: the opening lines of 'Auguries of Innocence' (in a slightly misquoted form) 'to see the world in a grain of sand' mark the entrance point to the mystery that constitutes the plot of the 2001 action movie *Lara Croft: Tomb Raider*. In a very different (and thoughtful) film, Johnny Depp plays a character called William Blake. *Dead Man*, written and directed by Jim Jarmusch, is not a portrayal of Blake himself, but uses his name and poetry to think through themes affecting present-day America.

SUMMARY

As this chapter indicates, there are no limits on how Blake can be appropriated. He is used by radicals and self-styled anti-institutionalists such as Huxley, Ginsberg and Jim Morrison, but he is also used by the institutions and authorities themselves. His face appeared on a 1958 Russian stamp and, in 1997, the year of Princess Diana's death, the Queen quoted Blake in her Christmas speech:

> Joy and sadness are part of all our lives. Indeed, the poet William Blake tells us that:
>
> 'Joy and woe are woven fine,
> A clothing for the soul divine,
> Under every grief and pine
> Runs a joy with silken twine.'
>
> This interweaving of joy and woe has been very much brought home to me and my family during the last months. We all felt the shock and sorrow of Diana's death.[4]

The diversity of Blake's meanings can be glimpsed in relation to the preface to *Milton*, the lines that have been turned into the hymn

'Jerusalem'. 'Jerusalem' is used in that bastion of English patriotism, the Last Night of the Proms, but more problematically it has also been appropriated by the far-right British National Party (who sell it as a ringtone on their website). It is the anthem of the (British) Women's Institute, it is played at English rugby and cricket matches, and it has been covered by a number of pop groups including Emerson, Lake, and Palmer. Presumably the meaning of Blake's words differ in each of these contexts, not only from each other, but also from the original function of the poem as a preface to one of Blake's prophecies. The fact is that Blake's works, both visual and poetic, often appear in contexts that seem not only irrelevant, but sometimes even antithetical to their original meanings. An example is the use of Blake by Donald Trump, one of America's most famous multi-millionaires:

> [T]he penthouse atop Donald Trump's 1 Central Park West complex boasts a "Library Dining Room" that features framed proverbs from *The Marriage of Heaven and Hell*, including "The road of excess leads to the palace of wisdom" and "You never know what is enough unless you know what is more than enough" (Goode, 769)

This is reported in an article that raises an important question of whether meanings can be maintained in relation to Blake's work when so much of it exists in a world of quotation. Goode looks at a range of such uses of Blake's 'Proverbs of Hell' and suggests:

> Given such varied invocations of Blake's proverb, one critical impulse is to try to show how they do violence to the proverb, how they uproot it from its historical and textual contexts to endorse ideologies inconsistent with the politics of *The Marriage of Heaven and Hell*, with Blake, or with 1790s British radicalism. Some version of this historicist impulse prompts our raised eyebrows or provokes our laughs when the radical anticapitalist Blake is apprenticed to endorse the Trump lifestyle. Yet it is difficult to defend the position that the proverb, once dislocated from Blake's copperplate and relocated onto the gilded walls of a luxury penthouse, cannot mean what Trump seems to want it to mean there. (Goode, 770)

There is, however, one area in which the meaning of Blake's works is certain: the art market. Blake is now, among other things, a commodity, and the major Blake journal, *Blake: An Illustrated Quarterly*, gives an annual review of the sales of his works. This is of course essential for Blake scholars, as it enables them to keep track of his works, but whether its significance ends there is not entirely clear. Blake scholar and co-editor of the Blake Archive, Robert Essick, is himself a major collector. His review entitled 'Blake in the Marketplace, 2004' listed that year's auction sales of Blake pieces, but Essick also called the sale of the print of *The Good and Evil Angels Struggling for Possession of a Child*, '[t]he blockbuster event of 2004' (Essick, 124). The print fetched $3.5 million which, as Essick notes, 'set a new record for any work by Blake, and I believe a record for any single print by any artist' (Essick, 124). There's an excitement registered here whereby the interests of professional Blake scholars come together with those of the auctioneers. It may be that Donald Trump's use of Blake's proverbs is not so inconsistent with the twenty-first-century meaning of Blake's work after all, but it nonetheless stands in stark contrast to Blake's own vision of art:

Where any view of Money exists Art cannot be carried on, but War only (*Laocoön*, E274)

STUDY QUESTIONS

1. In the light of this chapter and Chapter 4, how can we talk usefully about the 'meaning' of Blake's work?
2. Blake's principal criticism of his major artistic influences (such as the Bible and *Paradise Lost*) takes place by rewriting parts of those works. Can the appropriations of Blake discussed in this chapter be considered in the same light? Are they rewritings, and do they actually tell us anything about Blake?

CHAPTER 6

GUIDE TO FURTHER READING

COMPLETE WORKS: EDITIONS AND FACSIMILES

There are several editions of Blake's complete writings available, the standard edition is David Erdman's *The Complete Poetry and Prose of William Blake*, newly revised edition (Anchor Books, 1988) to which I have referred throughout this book.

INDIVIDUAL AND SELECTED WORKS: EDITIONS AND FACSIMILES

Beginning in the 1950s, the Trianon Press started to issue hand-coloured, hand-stencilled reproductions of Blake's illuminated works. These were expensive editions to begin with, and a copy of, say, *Jerusalem*, can cost thousands of pounds today. Fortunately, during the 1990s the Tate Gallery undertook production of a complete set of Blake's illuminated words. Alongside the reproductions are the text of the plates, and there is introductory material, critical discussion and summaries. There are six volumes which cost (in paperback) about £20–30 each, and are now published by Thames & Hudson. However, the colour plates from the entire set (with no accompanying critical text) are also available in a single volume for about the same price: *William Blake: The Complete Illuminated Books*, ed. David Bindman (London: Thames & Hudson, 2000). In terms of its reproductions, this collection supersedes David Erdman's *The Illuminated Blake* (New York: Doubleday, 1974), which also reproduces all of Blake's illuminated works in a single volume with the advantage of a plate-by-plate commentary, but with the disadvantage that the reproductions are all the same size (about

A5), and that they are all in black and white. The Erdman edition is published by Dover, who also provide a range of cheap reproductions of Blake's works in paperback, although the texts are not as reliable as, say, the Tate Gallery editions. For more reliable, cheaper, smaller facsimiles there are copies of *Songs of Innocence and of Experience*, and *The Marriage of Heaven and Hell*, both edited by Geoffrey Keynes and published by Oxford University Press (1970 and 1975 respectively). Also useful is S. Foster Damon's edition of Blake's illustrations to the Book of Job (entitled *Blake's Job*), as are the editions of *Urizen* and *Milton*, both edited by Kay and Roger Easson, although these are now out of print.

OTHER EDITIONS

For a selection of Blake with a more useful commentary than any of the complete writings discussed above, see David Fuller's *William Blake: Selected Poetry and Prose* (Harlow: Longman, 2000), which offers an excellent overview of Blake criticism and helpful introductions to each of the poems.

REPRODUCTIONS OF PAINTINGS AND NON-ILLUMINATED WORKS

A good selection of Blake's paintings is available in Raymond Lister's *Paintings of William Blake* (Cambridge: Cambridge University Press, 1986), and a selection of his pencil sketches can be found in *Drawings of William Blake* (New York: Dover, 1970), edited by Geoffrey Keynes.

ELECTRONIC RESOURCES

The resources here are excellent. http://www.english.uga.edu/wblake offers access to an online concordance, which has the advantage of being page-referenced to both Keynes and Erdman, as well as offering access to an electronic edition of Erdman's *Complete Poetry and Prose*. The Blake Archive (http://www.blakearchive.org) is a superb resource with very substantial financial and scholarly support. It contains colour facsimiles of all of Blake's illuminated books, along with many other materials.

Joseph Viscomi, author of *Blake and the Idea of the Book*, currently has many of his articles on Blake's working methods online at http://sites.unc.edu/viscomi/frontend_page.html

The impact of Blake on later artists is discussed in a list at the end of the article entitled 'William Blake' on the collaborative online encyclopedia, Wikipedia (http://en.wikipedia.org/wiki/William_Blake). The reliability of Wikipedia cannot be guaranteed, but this is an eclectic and interesting resource.

BIOGRAPHIES

There are many biographies of Blake. The earliest full account by Gilchrist is now in print again, with a helpful introduction by Richard Holmes: *Gilchrist on Blake* (London: HarperCollins, 2005). Peter Ackroyd has written a more recent popular biography, *Blake* (London: Sinclair-Stevenson, 1995), although the most scholarly, detailed and informed biography is *The Stranger from Paradise* (New Haven: Yale University Press, 2001) by Bentley, author of *Blake Records*. For a shorter biography that contains a greater degree of critical discussion of the works, try John Beer's *Blake: A Literary Life* (Basingstoke: Palgrave, 2005).

BLAKE AND RELIGION/THE BIBLE

A useful introduction to Blake's religious context can be found in Robert Ryan's chapter on Blake and Religion in *The Cambridge Companion to William Blake*, and further material in Robert Ryan's book *The Romantic Reformation* (Cambridge: Cambridge University Press, 1997). A detailed study of Blake's use of the Bible is to be found in Leslie Tannenbaum's *Biblical Tradition in Blake's Early Prophecies* (Princeton: Princeton University Press, 1992), and further discussion can be found in Erdman's edited collection of essays, *Blake and his Bibles* (Connecticut: Locust Hill Press, 1990). The discussion of Blake's theology in J. G. Davies's *The Theology of William Blake* (Oxford: Clarendon Press, 1948) presents a conservative assessment of the poet's theology, but for a radical vision of the same, see Thomas Altizer's *The New Apocalypse: The Radical Christian Vision of William Blake* (East Lansing: Michigan State University Press, 1967). For Blake's self-conception as a prophet, see Murray Roston's *Prophet and Poet* (London: Faber & Faber, 1965); for his engagement with apocalypse, see Paley's *Apocalypse and Millennium in English Romantic Poetry* (Oxford: Clarendon, 1999).

OTHER READING

In addition to the primary texts and works on Blake's religion listed above, I include below an unannotated bibliography on different aspects of Blake's work that have been touched on in this book.

Reference works

G. E. Bentley Jr, *Blake Records*, second edition (New Haven: Yale University Press, 2004)

S. Foster Damon, *A Blake Dictionary* (Providence: Brown University Press, 1965)

David Fuller, 'William Blake', in *Literature of the Romantic Period: A Bibliographical Guide*, ed. Michael O'Neill (Oxford: Clarendon, 1997)

Journals

Blake: An Illustrated Quarterly

Blake and the Body

Tristanne Connolly, *William Blake and the Body* (Basingstoke: Palgrave, 2002)

Thomas Frosch, 'The Risen Body', in Hazard Adams (ed.), *Critical Essays on William Blake* (Boston: G. K. Hall & co., 1991)

Jean Hagstrum, 'Christ's Body', in *William Blake: Essays in Honour of Sir Geoffrey Keynes* (Oxford: Clarendon Press, 1973)

Anne Mellor, *Blake's Human Form Divine* (Berkeley: University of California Press, 1974)

Alicia Ostriker, 'Desire Gratified and Ungratified', in *William Blake: Essays in Honour of Sir Geoffrey Keynes* (Oxford: Clarendon Press, 1973)

Blake's contexts

David Bindman, *William Blake: His Art and Times* (New Haven: Yale Center for British Art, 1982)

Steve Clark and David Worrall, *Historicizing Blake* (New York: St Martin's Press, 1994)

David Erdman, *Blake: Prophet against Empire* (Princeton: Princeton University Press, 1977)

Robert N. Essick and Donald Pearce (eds), *Blake in his Time* (Bloomington: Indiana University Press, 1978)

Jon Mee, *Dangerous Enthusiasm* (Oxford: Clarendon Press, 1992)

E. P. Thomson, *Witness Against the Beast* (Cambridge: Cambridge University Press, 1993)

Blake and empire/nationalism

Saree Makdisi, *William Blake and the Impossible History of the 1790s* (Chicago: University of Chicago Press, 2002)

Julia M. Wright, *Blake, Nationalism, and the Politics of Alienation* (Ohio: Ohio University Press, 2004)

Blake and feminism

Helen P. Bruder, *William Blake and the Daughters of Albion* (Basingstoke: Macmillan, 1997) – worth reading alongside the chapter 'Blake and Women' in Dent and Whittaker (see Works Cited).

Blake and human relationships

Michael Ferber, *The Social Vision of William Blake* (Princeton: Princeton University Press, 1985)

Christopher Z. Hobson, *Blake and Homosexuality* (Basingstoke: Palgrave, 2000)

Jeanne Moskal, *Blake, Ethics and Forgiveness* (Tuscaloosa: University of Alabama Press, 1994)

Blake and language

Nelson Hilton, *Literal Imagination* (Berkeley: California University Press, 1983)

Peter Otto, *Constructive Vision and Visionary Deconstruction* (Oxford: Clarendon Press, 1991)

Blake and Marxism

Judy Cox, *William Blake: The Scourge of Tyrants* (London: Redwords, 2004)

Blake and psychoanalysis/psychotherapy

Edward F. Edinger, *Encounter with the Self: A Jungian Commentary on William Blake's 'Illustrations of the Book of Job'* (Toronto: Inner City Books, 1986)

Diana Hume George, *Blake and Freud* (Ithaca: Cornell University Press, 1980)

Jerry Caris Godard, *Mental Forms Creating: William Blake Anticipates Freud, Jung, and Rank* (Lanham: University Press of America, 1985)

June Singer, *Blake, Jung and the Collective Unconscious* (York Beach: Nicolas-Hays, 2000)

Blake's reception history

Shirley Dent and Jason Whittaker, *Radical Blake: Influence and Afterlife from 1827* (Basingstoke: Palgrave, 2002)

Deborah Dorfman, *Blake in the Nineteenth Century* (New Haven: Yale University Press, 1969)

Mike Goode, 'Blakespotting', *PMLA*, 121:3 (2006), 769–86

Blake and Science

Donald Ault, *Visionary Physics* (Chicago: University of Chicago Press, 1974)

Blake's Sources

Kathleen Raine, *Blake and Tradition* (London: Routledge & Kegan Paul, 1969)

Blake's System/Mythology

C. A. Abrahams, *William Blake's Fourfold Man* (Bonn: Bouvier, 1978)

John Beer, *Blake's Humanism* (Manchester: Manchester University Press, 1968)

Leopold Damrosch, *Symbol and Truth in Blake's Myth* (Princeton: Princeton University Press,1980)

Northrop Frye, *Fearful Symmetry* (Princeton: Princeton University Press, 1947)

Blake's Style

William Kumbier, 'Blake's Epic Meter', *Studies in Romanticism*, 17 (1978), 163–92

Alicia Ostriker, *Vision and Verse in William Blake* (Madison & Milwaukee: University of Wisconsin Press, 1965)

Blake as visual artist, engraver and printmaker
Steve Clark and David Worrall, *Blake in the Nineties* (Basingstoke: Macmillan, 1999)

D. W. Dörrbecker, 'Innovative Reproduction', in Clark and Worrall (eds), *Blake in the Nineties* (discusses Blake and the Royal Academy)

Morris Eaves, *Blake's Theory of Art* (Princeton: Princeton University Press, 1982)

Robert N. Essick, *William Blake: Printmaker* (Princeton: Princeton University Press, 1980)

Joseph Viscomi, *Blake and the Idea of the Book* (Princeton: Princeton University Press, 1993)

Criticism of individual works
Stuart Curran (ed.), *Blake's Sublime Allegory: Essays on The Four Zoas, Milton and Jerusalem* (Madison: University of Wisconsin, 1973)

S. Foster Damon, *Blake's Job* (Providence: Brown University Press, 1967)

Morris Eaves (ed.), *The Cambridge Companion to William Blake* (Cambridge: Cambridge University Press, 2003) – has chapters on key works of different periods

Heather Glen, *Vision and Disenchantment: Blake's Songs and Wordsworth's Lyrical Ballads* (Cambridge: Cambridge University Press, 1983)

Morton Paley, *The Traveller in the Evening: The Last Works of William Blake* (Oxford: Oxford University Press, 2003)

Michael Phillips (ed.), *Interpreting Blake* (Cambridge: Cambridge University Press, 1973) – has separate chapters on the major works

See also the commentaries in the individual Tate Gallery volumes mentioned earlier.

Miscellaneous
John Adlard, *Sports of Cruelty: Folklore of William Blake* (London: Cecil and Amelia Woolf, 1972)

Steve Clark, '"Labouring at the Resolute Anvil": Blake's Response to Locke', in Clark and Worrall (eds), *Blake in the Nineties* (see Works Cited)

Vincent De Luca, *Words of Eternity: Blake and the Poetics of the Sublime* (Princeton: Princeton University Press, 1991)

Roger R. Easson, 'Blake and the Gothic', in Essick and Pearce (eds), *Blake in his Time* (see Works Cited)

Peter F. Fisher, 'Blake and the Druids', *Journal of English and Germanic Philology*, LVIII (1959), 589–612

Peter F. Fisher, 'Blake's Attacks on the Classical Tradition', *Philological Quarterly*, Jan., XL (1961), 1–18

Jean H. Hagstrum, 'William Blake Rejects the Enlightenment', in Hazard Adams (ed.), *Critical Essays on William Blake* (Boston: G. K. Hall & co., 1991)

Nelson Hilton, 'What has *Songs* to do with Hymns?' in Clark and Worrall (eds), *Blake in the Nineties* (see Works Cited)

David Wagenknecht, *Blake's Night: William Blake and the Idea of Pastoral* (Massachusetts: Harvard University Press, 1973)

Joseph A. Wittreich, *Angel of Apocalypse: Blake's Idea of Milton* (Madison: University of Wisconsin, 1975)

WORKS CITED

Barker, Kenneth L. (ed.), *NIV Study Bible: New International Version* (London: Hodder & Stoughton, 1998)

Bentley, G. E. Jr, *The Stranger from Paradise* (New Haven: Yale University Press, 2001)

Bentley, G. E. Jr, *Blake Records*, second edition (New Haven: Yale University Press, 2004)

Bindman, David, *William Blake: His Art and Times* (New Haven: Yale Center for British Art, 1982)

Burke, Edmund, *A Philosophical Enquiry into the Origin of our Ideas of the Sublime and Beautiful* (Oxford: Oxford University Press, 1990)

Clark, Steve and David Worrall (eds), *Historicizing Blake* (New York: St Martin's Press, 1994)

Clark, Steve and David Worrall (eds), *Blake in the Nineties* (Basingstoke: Macmillan, 1999)

Coggins, R. J. and J. L. Houlden (eds), *A Dictionary of Biblical Interpretation* (London: SCM, 1990)

Coleridge, Samuel Taylor, *The Complete Poems* (London: Penguin Classics, 1997)

Davies, Keri and Marsha Keith Schuchard, 'Recovering the Lost Moravian History of William Blake's Family', *Blake: An Illustrated Quarterly*, 38:1 (Summer 2004)

Dent, Shirley and Jason Whittaker, *Radical Blake: Influence and Afterlife from 1827* (Basingstoke: Palgrave, 2002)

Dorfman, Deborah, *Blake in the Nineteenth Century* (New Haven: Yale University Press, 1969)

T. S. Eliot: Selected Prose, ed. John Hayward (London: Penguin, 1953)

Eliot, T. S., *Collected Poems 1909–1962*, (London: Faber, 2002)

Erdman, David, *Blake: Prophet against Empire* (Princeton: Princeton University Press, 1977)

Erdman, David, *The Complete Poetry and Prose of William Blake*, newly revised edition (Anchor Books, 1988)

Essick, Robert, *William Blake: Printmaker* (Princeton: Princeton University Press, 1982)

Essick, Robert, 'Blake in the Marketplace, 2004', *Blake: An Illustrated Quarterly*, 38:4 (Summer 2005)

Essick, Robert and Donald Pearce (eds), *Blake in his Time* (Bloomington: Indiana University Press, 1978)

Frye, Northrop, *Fearful Symmetry* (Princeton: Princeton University Press, 1947)

Goode, Mike, 'Blakespotting', *PMLA*, 121:3 (2006), 769–86

Holmes, Richard, *Gilchrist on Blake* (London: HarperCollins, 2005)

Klonsky, Milton, *William Blake: The Seer and His Visions* (London: Orbis Books, 1977)

Mee, Jon, *Dangerous Enthusiasm* (Oxford: Clarendon Press, 1992)

Paine, Thomas, *Common Sense* (London: Penguin Classics, 1982)

Radcliffe, Ann, *The Mysteries of Udolpho* (Oxford: Oxford University Press, 1998)

Raine, Kathleen, *Blake and Tradition* (London: Routledge & Kegan Paul, 1969)

Roston, Murray, *Prophet and Poet* (London: Faber & Faber, 1965)

Ruskin, John, *Unto This Last* (London: Penguin Classics, 1986)

Shepherd, Jack, *In Lambeth* (London: Methuen, 1990)

Viscomi, Joseph, *Blake and the Idea of the Book* (Princeton: Princeton University Press, 1993)

Wu, Duncan, *Romanticism: An Anthology*, second edition (Oxford: Blackwell, 1988)

W. B. Yeats: Selected Criticism, ed. A. Norman Jeffares (London: Pan, 1976)

NOTES

CHAPTER 3

1   Due to the evolution of Blake's mythology, Los is not really the
    contrary of Urizen in the later works, and he represents imagina-
    tion rather than energy. Nonetheless, 'energy' is so strongly asso-
    ciated with artistic creativity in *The Marriage* that it is fair to
    align the two for illustrative purposes in Blake's work of this
    earlier period.

CHAPTER 5

1   http://books.guardian.co.uk/departments/classics/story/0,6000,
    386024,00.html
2   http://www.tarotgarden.com/library/articles/wmblaketarot.html
3   http://www.tate.org.uk/britain/exhibitions/blake/blakevents.htm
4   http://www.royal.gov.uk/output/Page4653.asp

INDEX